Parenting the ADD Child

Can't Do? Won't Do?

David Pentecost

Jessica Kingsley Publishers
London and Philadelphia

First published in the United Kingdom in 2000
by Jessica Kingsley Publishers
116 Pentonville Road
London N1 9JB, UK
and
400 Market Street, Suite 400
Philadelphia, PA 19106, USA

www.jkp.com

Copyright © David Pentecost 2000
Printed digitally since 2009

Library of Congress Cataloging in Publication Data

Pentecost, David, 1959–
    Parenting the ADD child: Can't Do? Won't Do? / David Pentecost.
      p. cm.
    Includes bibliographical references (p.   ) And index.
    1. Problem children--Behaviour modification. 2 Parenting.
    3. Attention-deficit-disordered children--Psychology. I. Title.
HQ773.P45   1999   99-43195
649'64--dc21   CIP

British Library Cataloguing in Publication Data

Pentecost, David
    Parenting the ADD child: Can't do? Won't do?
    1. Attention-deficit-disordered children - Care
    2. Attention-deficit hyperactivity disorder - Popular works
    I. Title
618.9'28589
ISBN 1 85302 811 8

ISBN 978 1 85302 811 3

Contents

ACKNOWLEDGEMENTS   8

1   Has Your Child got ADD?   9

2   ADD Alternative Parenting Techniques   17

3   Why Not Just Take Pills?   21

4   What Does ADDapt Do?   25

5   Don't be Hard on Yourself!   29

6   Be Prepared to Change   33

7   Stick With It and Be Patient   37

8   Be Consistent   41

The ADDapt Programme

Step 1   *Keeping on Task — Powerful Motivators*   45

Step 2   *Who's the Boss? 'Special Time' — a New Approach*   51

Step 3   *The Home Points System: Part 1*   65

Step 4   *Praise — Your Secret Weapon*   75

Step 5   *Tackling Attention-Seeking*   83

Step 6   *The Secret of Commands*   93

Step 7   *Task Wars*   103

Step 8   *Mastering Things-to-Do*   111

Step 9   *The Home Points System: Part 2*   *119*

Step 10   *Time Out for Difficult Behaviours: Part 1*   *127*

Step 11   *Time Out for Difficult Behaviours: Part 2*   *135*

Step 12   *Putting It All Together*   *143*

APPENDIX 1 WORKING IN PARTNERSHIP   149
APPENDIX 2 SPECIAL TIME FOR OLDER CHILDREN   153
APPENDIX 3 SUPPORT GROUPS   157
APPENDIX 4 SUGGESTED READING AND WEBSITES   161

SUBJECT INDEX   165
AUTHOR INDEX   171

To Martha and Louis

Acknowledgements

The inspiration for this book and the ideas and approaches contained in it have many sources. There are people I want to thank for insights or ideas who may not be aware of their influence on what I wanted to write. My thanks to all of you.

I wish to thank my colleague Tony Ferguson who started the ADD development project with me and contributed much to my early thinking about this programme; Dr Kabir Padamsee who secured the funding and has supported us throughout; Suzanne Ferris for her work with the children and her comments on the manuscript; and the team at Raphael House whose versatility in the family work they do and whose dedication I continue to respect and admire.

I also want to thank all the families who gave me an opportunity to share my ideas, tried them out and were good enough to give me the feedback when I asked for it.

Thanks also to the many parents and children who shared their stories with me and trusted me with their problems, and whose lives and endeavours inspired me to write this book.

Thanks to Klaas Lageveen for the cover illustration, and to Rainer and Claus at d Rex for their work on the illustrations.

Finally, I want to express my deepest gratitude to two people whose labour and support enabled me to write this book. One of those is Mike Crook, who has been a source of strength and encouragement throughout. Our collaboration has come a long way since my first tentative request to him to 'take a look at this book I'm writing on ADD'. His contribution to the drafts and redrafts has been immense. Thanks to Mike's keen eye on the text and sound advice whenever I wanted it, the book reads the way I always wanted it to. Kindness, generosity and laughter have also been a part of his contribution to our work together.

And I thank Sue, my wife, for her patience and encouragement. She has done everything else that needed doing in the family while I have been writing. Her hard work and support have made this book possible.

CHAPTER I

Has Your Child Got ADD?

In this book you will read about children like Harry, Molly, Jamie and Simon.

Molly is a bright, intelligent five-year-old who is so active and defiant that her behaviour regularly reduces her mother to tears. She has broken all the furniture in her bedroom. She has broken windows throughout the house. She has threatened her mother with a knife. She has run away from home and was brought back by the police, who found her in the park.

Simon is ten. He also is bright, and at school they say he is above average and well ahead of most of his peers. But the school has also told his parents that Simon needs special learning support in class, hates working and has a chip on his shoulder. He has stolen from his teacher and his classmates. He has sworn at the headmaster in assembly and locked himself in the toilets, refusing to come out.

Jamie is seven. His parents have nicknamed him 'the boss'. This is no joke. He rules their lives with his constant demands and will stop at nothing so as to remain the centre of attention. He injures himself frequently as a result of the risks he takes. He first broke an arm falling from a tree when he was three. He has broken it twice more since then. He fractured his leg when he ran in front of a car, and broke three fingers fighting. He has been cautioned by the police for throwing bottles on to the motorway. He has few clothes because he regularly ruins them by deliberately cutting holes in them. He has never been invited to a party. He has no friends. Other children both fear and despise him.

Harry, six, can be a loving, caring boy when he is not demanding or flying into a spiteful, aggressive rage. His mother Helen believes she cannot control him. Six months ago he broke his three-year-old brother's nose with a cricket bat. Recently he kicked and punched Helen in the stomach so hard that she had to go to the local casualty department. She was pregnant at the time.

Soon after this Harry's parents spoke to the social services department, asking for him to be taken into care.

What do these children have in common?

1. They are all a parenting nightmare.

2. They have challenged the best attempts of their parents to change them.

3. They have all been referred to professionals by their parents.

4. I have met them all and helped their parents transform extreme behaviour into the kind one might reasonably expect from other children of their ages.

5. They have all been diagnosed as having a condition called Attention Deficit Disorder or ADD.

You may have a child with similar behaviour problems to those of Harry, Molly, Simon or Jamie, albeit not as severe. Someone may have suggested that your child has some of the symptoms of this disorder. Your GP may have mentioned it as a possibility, to explain the problems you are having. A psychiatrist may have diagnosed your child as having ADD. Wherever you come in this picture, you need to know about ADD, how it affects behaviour, and what can help.

ADD = inattention + impulsiveness

So what is ADD, and does your child have it? ADD is often spotted when a child behaves consistently badly and in extreme ways. Parents become aware of the way these behaviours set their children apart from others of the same age. Teachers spot how the behaviours set them apart from classmates.

Molly, Simon and Jamie show different types of extreme behaviour. However, they share a common diagnosis of ADD because similar patterns are found to underlie their behaviour. Identifying these common underlying patterns helps us to understand and treat them. The behaviours that make up ADD are grouped into two main areas: inattention and impulsiveness. In an ADD child both characteristics are present to some degree, but the precise mix will vary from child to child.

Inattention

One of the first things their parents noticed about Simon and Molly was their unusually short attention spans. They were always so much more easily distracted than the other children in their class and nursery group. They simply could not concentrate on tasks in the same way. As a result, they both started doing badly in their schoolwork and disrupting others.

Impulsiveness

What has been most noticeable about Jamie, on the other hand, is that he has always been a risk taker, always acting before thinking and seemingly blind to the consequences. His parents feel he does not learn from experience because he can't pause long enough to reflect before he acts. His parents first had Jamie tested for hearing problems because, in their words, 'He just didn't seem to hear us.' However, Jamie's hearing was perfect. ADD was the problem.

ADHD = inattention + impulsiveness + hyperactivity

Hyperactivity

What first struck Harry's mother, comparing him to her other children, was that as soon as he could walk he was always 'on the go' – impossible to keep up with. Now, at six, if he is not literally climbing the walls, he is never still, whether fidgeting, tapping his fingers or feet, swinging his legs or just wriggling. He is constantly up and down, usually doing several things at once, and he can never settle at mealtimes.

Harry has ADHD – Attention Deficit Hyperactivity Disorder. The term ADHD is sometimes used interchangeably with ADD, but strictly speaking they are different, although related, disorders. In addition to the impulsiveness and short attention spans which characterise ADD, ADHD children are hyperactive. However, the overall behavioural problems associated with the two conditions are very similar. Parents of ADHD children will find my parenting techniques extremely effective, even though throughout this book I will refer to ADD.

Every ADD child is different

ADD children share some symptoms but not all. For instance, Molly lacks concentration but isn't noisy; Jamie can play well with a jigsaw puzzle for short periods but shouts the whole time; Harry is a fidget but can concentrate on a game for hours; Simon can be still but seems in a dream world.

However, an ADD child is likely to show most if not all of the following traits:

- often fails to give close attention to details and makes careless mistakes

- often has difficulty sustaining attention in what he or she is doing

- often seems not to listen when spoken to directly

- often seems not to follow through on instructions and fails to finish tasks

- often has difficulty in organising tasks and activities

- often avoids or tries to get out of doing tasks that require sustained mental effort

- often loses things

- is often distracted

- is often forgetful in daily activities

- often fidgets with her hands or feet or squirms in his seat

- often leaves his seat in the classroom or in other situations where staying seated is expected

- often runs about or climbs over things when this is inappropriate

- often has difficulty playing quietly

- is often on the go or acts as if driven by a motor

- often talks non-stop

- often blurts out answers before questions have been completed

- often has difficulty waiting for her turn

- often interrupts or intrudes on others; butts into conversations or games.

ADD is more common than many people might think. Researchers have identified it in every nation and culture they have studied. In Britain, where the diagnosis is still expanding, conservative estimates suggest that as many as 5 in 100 children have it. Many studies estimate that between 2 and 9 per cent of all school-age children worldwide have ADD. Boys with ADD outnumber girls by 3 to 1.

What you need to know

- The behaviour patterns that typify ADD usually emerge between the ages of three and five, although some children don't develop them until late childhood or even early adolescence.

- The condition can last into and through adulthood.

- ADD children frequently experience problems making friends and sustaining relationships. They often suffer from low self-esteem as a consequence (see Step 4).

- Children with ADD need special parenting techniques with far greater attention paid to consistency than other children (see Chapter 7).

- There is no cure for ADD – although Ritalin and related drugs can reduce some of the symptoms (dramatically in many cases).

- No one knows for sure what causes ADD. There are a number of different theories. The most likely causes lie in the brain, specifically the actions of chemicals like Dopamine which have a role in inhibiting impulsive behaviour and influencing the ability to concentrate (see the article by R.A. Barkley listed on p.161 of this book).

- ADD is taken very seriously in the scientific and medical communities. Every month research throws more light on our understanding of it.

- Diagnosis of ADD is difficult. As yet there is no blood test or brain scan to confirm the condition. All our lives would be simpler if there were.

Help! This thing is crushing me!

- Like all behavioural disorders, ADD is very complex. There will be some similarities among ADD children but there may also be big differences. The mix and the severity of symptoms vary widely.

- A broken arm is a broken arm, but ADD can be more elusive. Your child may behave really badly most of the time, then be a perfect angel for that brief time when you are with the doctor or specialist. This also hampers the process of diagnosis.

- The growing number of diagnoses of ADD does not mean the condition is widely understood in society at large or even among all professionals. Too many people still believe that ADD is a myth, that it does not really exist as a condition. ADD children still risk getting stuck with the labels 'bad' or 'naughty'. Their parents risk getting labelled 'inadequate' or 'neglectful'. This labelling is grossly unfair and can have terrible consequences (see Chapter 4).

- Medication is regarded by many as the treatment of choice for ADD. But medication often has only moderate success with the associated behavioural problems. Alongside drug therapy, behavioural training (such as the programme set out in this book) is increasingly seen as an essential companion to drug therapy (see Chapters 2 and 3).

- Support groups for parents with a child with ADD and ADHD are growing around the country. Many parents find them an essential lifeline (see Step 12 and Appendix 3).

This book will not tell you all there is to know about ADD and its related conditions like ADHD. It gives you as much background information as you need to follow the programme, but no more than is strictly necessary. There are many excellent books around which go further into the theories about what is happening in ADD. Some you have probably read. My suggestions for further reading are found on page 161.

Together we will get to grips with it

Let me congratulate you for setting out on what should be an exciting, if arduous, journey. We are now emerging from the time when the professional always knew best into an age when professionals and their clients can be collaborators – sharing knowledge and insights along the way. I believe the potential for this type of collaboration and mutual respect is especially strong in areas like ADD. So welcome to the informal society of those committed to finding better ways of helping children with this condition.

Read on to discover what this book offers you.

CHAPTER 2

ADD Alternative Parenting Techniques

I have worked in the field of child and adolescent psychiatry for over ten years. A large part of this time has been spent helping parents who have a child with ADD. I am all too well aware of the frustrations and agonies they experience. They come to see me worn to a frazzle by the behaviour of their child, and they usually feel they are to blame. The children feel bad too. They arrive feeling labelled as uncontrollable and naughty. They lack self-confidence and self-esteem.

Often the family as a whole is at crisis point, each member blaming the others for creating the problem although each may secretly fear that it may all be his or her fault.

Parents with ADD children are people searching for solutions. They are desperately in need of support and understanding. The reason I have spent the last ten years helping them and have written this book is that I know things can change for them, and change rapidly.

Why *you* might need this book

Getting the right help for parenting an ADD child can be difficult. This is certainly true of England, which I know best, but I suspect it applies in other countries too. Medication is available but some doctors will not prescribe it. Professional help aimed at giving you extra parenting techniques is scarce. Getting the right help can be a lottery that depends on where you live.

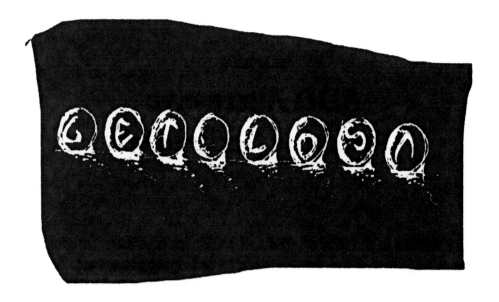

Lottery of help with ADD

Hence this book. It will give you the know-how to make lasting changes in your child's behaviour. In the pages that follow you will find solutions to the behaviour problems common with ADD. The programme I offer you I have christened **ADDapt – ADD Alternative Parenting Techniques.** You could call it training, education or behaviour modification, but it all comes down to special parenting techniques that will gradually and gently get your child to behave in the way you want. You, as parents, are the best people to help your ADD children change.

Why ADDapt will work for you

ADD children need different kinds of parenting – different, that is, from the ways that come, so to speak, 'naturally'. Parents need to know what works best with very difficult children. This is where ADDapt comes in. For example, ADDapt begins by making changes in the quality of the relationship between you and your ADD child – which may have taken a battering. As the programme progresses you will learn how to build his or her self-esteem; how to praise and reward effectively; how to reduce conflicts; how to tackle discipline issues, and so on.

The 12 steps of the ADDapt programme help the ADD child acquire new and good habits and to *unlearn* old and bad ones.

ADDapt leads to big reductions in:

- disruptive behaviour
- your child wanting your instant attention all the time
- spitefulness, fighting and aggression.

ADDapt leads to big improvements in:

- completing routine tasks
- waiting turns
- self-confidence
- relationships with peers and siblings.

Most important of all, parents report that ADDapt has helped to rebuild the harmony that has all too often been shattered during the ADD years.

ADDapt – not just for ADD

Although primarily for parents with an ADD child, many of the techniques in this book have proved equally helpful in parenting children with other behaviour problems, especially ADHD.

How this book supports you

This book is designed to be easy to follow, jargon-free, empowering and practical, so that you can produce the necessary change yourself. This way you become the 'expert'. At each step you are shown the techniques you need – what they are, why they work, how to use them – and the benefits you can expect to see both immediately and in the longer term. Because it assumes you are following the programme without outside support, much of the book deals with ways you can support yourself and give yourself strength and encouragement through all the hard work and the temporary setbacks.

How to use this book

A great deal of thought has been given to the tasks and exercises set out here. The order in which you complete the steps is important.

I can appreciate that you may be itching to get straight to issues that bother you most. There is always a temptation to skip the sections in self-help books that seem less relevant. I've done it myself. However, every part of ADDapt has a purpose. Do try not to skip. But if you do, you may find it useful to go back to the skipped sections if your morale begins to flag or if you feel you have lost your way. You may also find it useful to do this in any case. Each section has been designed to be reread whenever you feel the need.

There is no timescale for completing ADDapt. Every family is different. You are the best judge of when to move on to the next step of the programme. Go at your own pace. If you hit a block in one part of ADDapt, don't give up. Just carry on and come back to it later.

CHAPTER 3

Why Not Just Take Pills?

This chapter explains what you can generally expect from medication and why I believe medication is a part, *but only a part,* of a complete approach to ADD. Although in the preceding chapter I made some big claims for ADDapt, I am not suggesting you should use the programme without medication. Some of the best results are achieved when ADDapt and medication are used together.

What medication can do

The causes underlying the hard-to-live-with behaviour of ADD children are now widely believed to stem from the way their brains function. Researchers are finding more and more evidence that the brains of ADD children are different in subtle ways from those of other children, containing either too much or too little of certain chemicals. These subtle brain differences seem to make ADD children more easily distracted, impatient, unsettled, restless and overactive, and less likely to think through the consequences of their actions than other children of their age.

Drugs like Ritalin and Dexedrine are prescribed to correct these chemical differences in the brain. They often bring a rapid improvement in the ability to listen, concentrate, pay attention, focus on tasks, play constructively. The changes can be quite dramatic. The drugs can also sometimes have an effect on aggressive outbursts and temper tantrums.

The limitations of medication

Drugs commonly improve some aspects of a child's behaviour, but rarely all. The main limitation of medication is that it does not usually stop all 'naughty' behaviour.

Many parents experience enormous relief when drug treatment starts. Hope returns. However, in my experience this initial optimism can turn to despair when the behavioural problems that were driving them to distraction do not disappear.

The example of the Grant family is typical – Harry's mother Helen said:

After being diagnosed as having ADD, Harry was given Ritalin. It had a big impact on him – his ability to remember things, and sit still without getting ants in his pants. He just seemed calmer. But in other ways there was no change. We had the same old battles. The tablets had no effect on his constantly demanding attention, his spitefulness to his brother, always having to come first, and lashing out with his fists and kicking when he wanted his own way.

The worst aspects of a child's behaviour may escape the impact of the medication because they have become deeply ingrained *habits*. Harry, for instance, has *learned* ways to 'fight' the situations he doesn't like. Even with the medication making him more able to concentrate and remember things, he is likely to continue to fight until he *learns* other ways of behaving.

Medication can enable children to concentrate for longer and learn better. But they have to be helped to learn new ways of behaving and to unlearn the old, disruptive ones.

How ADD has affected your child

Many of the problems you experience with your ADD child arise from his or her difficulty in learning life's rules. We have all had to learn how to behave at mealtimes. We have all had to learn that we cannot have our own way all the time and that other people are not always able to attend to our needs instantly. And we have had to learn that other people too have needs that are just as important to them as ours are to us, and so on.

ADD causes children to be more impulsive, more inattentive and more hyperactive than other children, and these traits make it much harder for them to learn the lessons they need to learn to get along with other people. Pills cannot teach skills and rules – what they *can* do, though, is calm children down so that they can learn more easily. *But they do still have to learn. And this is where ADDapt works, in combination with medication, to provide the training that pills have now made possible.*

In short, my approach is to combine the best of both worlds.

The ADD drug debate

There are some practitioners who would argue that medication alone is the answer and who will continue to try different drugs and dosages in an attempt to get all aspects of behaviour under control. However, in my experience this can lead to overprescribing, with increased dangers of side-effects. I believe it is a mistake to expect drugs to do everything.

On the other hand, when parents who are apprehensive about giving drugs to their child ask me, 'Is medication really the quickest and most effective way of ensuring that my child's concentration and attention span will improve?', my answer has to be 'Yes'. Given everything that we currently

know from research and clinical experience, it is clear that medication can create the conditions for new parenting techniques to succeed.

Some parents are so pleased with the effects of medication that they feel nothing else is needed. If medication alone works for your child, fine. ADDapt is not for you. But if, despite the drugs, your relationship with your child is still an uphill battle, then ADDapt has plenty to offer you.

Table 3.1 What drugs do and don't do on their own		
Likely to change substantially: Abilities and traits	Likely to change to some extent	Unlikely to change much: Learned behaviour
• Poor concentration • Unstructured behaviour • Ability to pay attention • Ability to listen • Ability to play constructively • Ability to focus on tasks • Ability to listen to what you are saying • Ability to follow through tasks • Forgetfulness	• Impulsiveness • Hyperactivity • Frustration outbursts	• Attention-seeking • Defiance • Severe aggression and spitefulness • Destructiveness • Verbal abuse • 'Chip on the shoulder' • Anti-social behaviour • Temper tantrums

CHAPTER 4

What Does ADDapt Do?

In this chapter I will explain more about what you can expect from ADDapt and what ADDapt will expect from you.

The programme is based on four principles:

1. You, as a parent, are best placed to have the most influence on the behaviour of your ADD child (even if you are using medication to make the job easier).

2. Changing your child's behaviour is possible – when you know how.

3. Rewards, encouragement and explanation are the keys to change.

4. You too will have to learn some new skills and habits

How does ADDapt work?

ADDapt starts from where you are now. It recognises that you and your child have been through a lot and that probably you have all – you, your child, your partner and anyone else involved – had your confidence dented. Although I shall be asking you to take another look at some of the ways you have been dealing with your ADD child, ADDapt never assumes that you are a bad parent or that you are to blame for your child's condition or naughty behaviour.

ADDapt contains tried and tested methods. It aims to proceed from strength to strength and from positive outcome to positive outcome. It builds on successes and on a growing confidence in you and your child, and aims to keep *the conflict* between you at as low a level as possible. ADDapt never asks you to set goals that are unrealistic for an ADD child to achieve.

The backbone of ADDapt is **reward, encouragement** and **explanation**. The programme works on finding new ways of enjoying time together as a way of reminding you all how much you still care for each other and enjoy each other's company. Improving your relationship with your child is an important part of ADDapt, which goes hand in hand with improving her behaviour.

ADDapt gives you practical ways of helping your ADD child to know and remember exactly what she has to do.

ADDapt develops the art of praising and rewarding. Praise and rewards are *the single most important factors* in turning around the behaviour problems of ADD. Praise is your secret weapon.

The programme is not about harshness or rigid control. Punishment is not a major feature of the ADDapt approach, although it recognises that there are times when you have to be firm and assertive – and it empowers you to be firm and assertive when necessary. ADDapt gives you lots of ways of giving yourself support and of standing firm when your child resists change.

Most important, ADDapt gives you ways to make the whole process fun.

You've got what it takes

You don't have to be an Einstein to follow ADDapt. Nor do you need a qualification in psychiatry, psychology or psychotherapy. You have all the qualities and qualifications it takes to create change and achieve success.

If you are a loving and committed parent, keen to see your child's prospects improve, eager to get closer to her and determined to get her behaviour under control, then you have all you need and more. My advice is to believe in yourself and trust your ability to bring about change. Remember, if you have coped with your child so far you can cope with ADDapt.

ADDapt works!

ADDapt is a challenge, but I can promise you that the rewards of perseverance will be worth the effort. However unalterable your child's behaviour has seemed till now, change is possible. *The past does not equal the future.*

What ADDapt expects from you

The key to success with this programme is based on four Golden Rules. You need to start thinking about these before you begin ADDapt, and then *you need to stick to them* while following the programme's 12 steps.

The four Golden Rules are:

1. **Don't be hard on yourself!**

2. **Be prepared to change.**

3. **Stick with it and be patient.**

4. **Be consistent.**

These are important factors, so let me cover each in detail. My aim in doing so is simple: it is to get you thinking in the right way so that you can start on the right foot and make the most of ADDapt.

The Golden Rules

Chapters 5 to 8 are intended to set you up to succeed with ADDapt. They set out the four Golden Rules that are crucial to success. Feel free to return to these chapters any time, but especially if your morale starts to flag or you feel you are losing your way.

CHAPTER 5

Don't be Hard on Yourself!

Golden Rule No. 1: Don't be hard on yourself!

Blaming yourself and feeling guilty and a failure will not help you on this journey. ADDapt is a demanding enough road without carrying a rucksack full of guilt. Every time you need reminding of this, read this section again.

Guilt – there's a lot of it about

I have yet to meet a parent of an ADD child who has not at some point felt guilty about his or her parenting. Parents tell me that they often blame themselves and have also felt blamed by others for their child's behaviour problems. They often feel the problems stem from them even to the point that they worry that they may have 'passed' the ADD to their child.

Feeling guilty won't help

If you feel at fault it doesn't help your morale. On a programme like ADDapt where you need to believe in yourself and believe that you can succeed, these guilty feelings get in the way of taking action and impede your ability to follow through. The biggest danger when it comes to self-blame and guilt is that they may prevent you from generating the determination and singlemindedness it takes to put a programme like this into action and go the distance.

False messages

So where do the guilt feelings come from and how can you neutralise them? There are a lot of myths and negative ideas around about the parents of ADD children. It is these that generate a lot of the self-blame and guilt. Here are some common **false beliefs** about ADD:

1. The parents of ADD children have no idea how to control their children.

2. Children have ADD problems because their parents cannot work together as parents.

3. The parents of ADD children always blame their child, never themselves.

4. The parents of ADD children have no insight into the things they are doing wrong.

5. The parents of ADD children probably experienced bad parenting.

6. The parents of ADD children look for ADD because they haven't got the skills to parent properly.

Anyone who believes any of the above myths is not living in the real world. Every one of the families I have worked with has had one or more of the above said about them – sometimes dressed up in professional jargon that basically means the same thing: 'You are to blame!' How, I ask myself, are parents meant to feel when they hear this misinformation? Is it going to make them feel empowered and give them faith in themselves and in their abilities to change their child? Of course not.

Few people who have not been faced with the problem can appreciate just how disruptive and difficult an ADD child can be. An ADD child can make you tired, irritable, frustrated and on a permanently short fuse. These emotions are brought on by the demands of the child's behaviour. They in turn may affect your behaviour towards your child. You and your child may both then become stuck in a vicious circle of confrontation and conflict. All this can produce guilt – particularly when you see yourself saying and doing things to your child which you know you shouldn't.

But this does not make you a bad parent – just a normal parent under extreme stress. Being snappy and negative about your child is *symptomatic* of the ADD situation, *not* the cause of it.

You are not to blame

In my clinical work I have found that the truth is precisely the opposite of all these myths.

The parents I see are good, capable people who have their child's interests at heart. They do not differ from other parents in their level of skills, tolerance or patience. They are simply facing tougher problems than most because *ADD can be a parenting nightmare.* Parenting an ADD child can place *extreme* stress on a family. Parents don't experience the rewards of seeing their child do as he is told, learn by example or respond to normal praise. Over the last ten years I have been amazed by the tenacity and patience that parents have shown with children whose behaviour would test a saint!

'Normal' good parenting just doesn't work on ADD kids. Their parents need extra-special skills to manage their behaviour, but it is not the parents' fault if they don't have them. I look at it this way … when your baby was born you were not to know that you were going to have to learn all you now know about ADD. An ADD child's tendency to be overactive, to do things without thinking, to require constant reminders, to appear not to listen, to forget

Typical parent of an ADD child

something that he was told two minutes earlier, to act on his impulses even though he has been told a hundred times not to, make it impossible to use the usual ways of parenting in a positive way.

How to stop feeling guilty

What parents need to hear is what they are doing right.

Think about all the things *you* are doing right. First, you love your child. I believe that the battles between ADD children and their parents are almost always an expression of love on the part of the parents. For example, parents insist on things like talking quietly, not fidgeting and not running about so as to ensure their child's acceptance in the world of adults – where, rightly or wrongly, people will judge children by such things. Giving children an experience of discipline and limits is a way of helping them develop self-control. It is a *loving* act. A child needs to know that showing respect for others gets respect in return.

Second, you have stuck by your child. Because few people understand the full extent of ADD behaviour they judge too quickly. Very few parents of ADD children are ever given the credit they are due for having coped as well as they have; for not having given up – though they may well have been tempted to. In difficult circumstances, you are still battling to make changes for the sake of your child and your family.

Third, you have taken a major step forward by reading this book and being motivated to 'have a go'. You will have done even better if you take action and persevere and make real progress. The programme will help you to achieve this.

Last, you are equipping yourself to become an expert on handling ADD.

TIPS FOR SUCCESS

- Believe in yourself.

- Trust in your ability to bring about change.

- Remember that you have all the qualifications you need to turn this problem around. Your motto from now on should be: 'The past does not equal the future.'

- Need reminding of this? Read this section again whenever you catch yourself giving yourself a hard time.

CHAPTER 6

Be Prepared to Change

Golden Rule No. 2: Be prepared to change

ADDapt is about change – change in the way you and your child behave. This kind of change is always hard. I am asking you to face the challenge of doing things differently.

However, I cannot stress enough that asking you to change does not imply that you have been a terrible parent or an inadequate person. And the fact that I am asking you to try some new ways of doing things does not mean I think you have been stupid or negligent because you are not doing them already. ADD takes a lot out of parents. The child's defiant behaviour is often well 'over the top'. It is natural that you should have lost confidence in some aspects of your parenting and particularly in your ability to create change. After all, you probably feel you have been trying to do this for years with little success. Don't worry – once you know exactly what to do you will be able to make progress.

But if you are still hearing those negative messages, then I suggest you reread Chapter 5, 'Don't be Hard on Yourself!'

ADDapt and the problem of change

ADDapt can change your life – providing you apply it with dedication and persistence. You will have been striving to achieve change for some time, and a desire for change is probably the reason you are reading this book. However, all too often, parents get discouraged when the first setbacks and hiccups occur. I have looked closely at the reasons why they falter when it comes to making the real changes they need. I have interviewed families to find out what happened in the first weeks of the programme, and the results have been very revealing. Three factors, it seems, contribute to parents dropping out early on:

- ambivalent feelings about the ADD diagnosis

- parents having problems working together

- parents clinging to the old ways of disciplining and punishing their children.

The basics that you need to have in place right now

I now need you, armed with your new knowledge, to make three important changes – if you have not already done so – in order to get the most out of ADDapt.

1. Accept that ADD has changed the lives of you and your child

I want you to fully accept the idea that your child has ADD. If either you or your partner secretly believes that ADD is not a disorder but the result of bad parenting, it will be hard to embrace fully the ADDapt programme. If anyone in the family harbours the belief that nothing is really wrong or that the fault lies with the child – 'He's just a devious, attention-seeking brat who needs a good hiding', for example – he or she will cling to old ways of responding which usually mean applying harsher discipline and making critical comments.

2. Work together

ADDapt needs all the adults in the life of the child to create and maintain a united front. If you are parenting with someone and you don't see eye to eye on the points raised by ADDapt, it will be hard to work together. If you don't work together, ADDapt may not work at all. Disagreements will increase the tension and conflict. If this is a likely problem area for you, you need to look at it *now.* Appendix 1, 'Working in Partnership', specifically addresses these issues, covers the problems in detail and offers strategies that will help.

3. Be prepared to give up your old ways of disciplining

If your old ways of disciplining and punishing your child were going to work, they would have done so by now! Many parents resort to smacking and shouting as their way of teaching children about rules, but ADD children can find themselves receiving more than their fair share of both.

Parents who have used ADDapt tell me that it makes them aware of just how critical and punitive their parenting had become. This realisation can feel uncomfortable. Try not to allow guilt to take over (see Chapter 5). These guilty feelings can hold you back from taking action. Always remember, you were doing the best you could.

The best action you can take to neutralise your guilty feelings at this stage is to *put your old strategies to one side and experiment with new ones.* It will mean cutting down on smacks, shouting, punishments and arguments. This can be hard. Some of the alternatives I offer may at first glance seem rather strange, but don't judge them too quickly. Please give them a try – and see how effective they can be!

ADD children and change: Expect resistance

I warn you now that **your child is going to resist change**. Change brings conflict. Although I have organised ADDapt to keep the conflict to a minimum and to give you tools for dealing with it, conflict there will certainly be. There will be times when you feel the programme is taking you backwards rather than forwards; sticking with it and being patient are what you need (see Chapter 7).

TIPS FOR SUCCESS

- To tackle the problem of ADD, the first and most important rule is to be flexible and open to new ideas.

- Admit that there is a problem with your child – and its name is ADD – which he or she cannot help and that you on your own have been unable to solve.

- Prepare to give up your existing ways of disciplining your child and be ready to accept new ones.

- Get your co-parent (if you have one) to commit to working with you as a united team.

Decisions exercise

Before embarking on another change, it can be helpful to reflect on successful changes you have made in the past.

Try to describe one or two good decisions to change that you have made – setting up your own home, buying a house, finding the best school for your child – and write down how you succeeded in that task. You will be surprised how impressive it looks on paper. Try telling a friend or partner, or just spend some time thinking about it.

Whichever you choose, list for yourself: how you overcame obstacles, what it took from you to make these changes, how you avoided losing your resolve, and how you managed to follow through your ideas into action.

Decision 1 . . . .

. . . .

. . . .

. . . .

. . . .

. . . .

. . . .

. . . .

Decision 2 . . . .

. . . .

. . . .

. . . .

. . . .

. . . .

. . . .

. . . .

CHAPTER 7

Stick With It and Be Patient

Golden Rule No. 3: Stick with it and above all be patient

The secret of success lies in persistence: sticking to it day in, day out; hour by hour. ADDapt will help you, I promise, but even with ADDapt's tried and tested methods parents often report setbacks and losses of faith on the road to success. If you lose heart, if you stop and start, the programme will be less effective and your child will become very confused.

'This book can change your life'

How many times have you read that on the back of a self-help book? Actually, it seems that 70 per cent of self-help books of all kinds – from dieting to building a new career – are not even read through to the end. These books aren't badly written or misguided. People begin them with the best intentions but then lose interest and stop reading.

Change of any kind, from losing weight to stopping smoking, takes dedicated, persistent application and all of us find it hard to break old habits. Just reading a book – even all the way through! – is not enough; hiccups and setbacks are an inevitable part of change.

No slacking off

There will always be a real temptation to stop the programme when things start to improve – it's human nature. Resist it. Your child may beg you to give up the programme with the promise that he will be good. The choice is yours, but remember, changing direction after a positive start is very confusing for him. It will give the impression that you cannot make changes in your behaviour and stick to them. This is not the example you want to set.

I've no doubt that there will be times when you will tackle tasks with vigour and enthusiasm and others when you will be dispirited and half-hearted. In truth, this doesn't matter. What matters most is that *your child sees you endure and carry through your ideas* when it would be much easier to stop.

Be patient

Sticking at it when change seems terribly slow in coming is the real challenge. Change will not come overnight, and all of you will have to get used to new ideas and to giving up old ways.

Beware of the inner voice encouraging you to backslide

Be especially wary when the voices telling you to backslide are the loudest. For instance:

- when you've had a long day with the kids or at work
- when no one seems to understand how hard it is for you
- when you have loads to do and no time for yourself.

Times like these, when you most feel like giving up, may hold the key to your ability to make a fresh start. Look at the examples I've just given. Frustration and despair are the main feelings being generated at such moments. These feelings do funny things to one's judgement. In my clinical experience many parents give up just at the point when they were about to turn the corner in making progress with their child. Often the really tough ground work has been done and the misery endured, but frustration and despair evoke reactions in us that cloud our judgement so we miss the small signs that things are beginning to shift. Try to use the feelings of wanting to give up as a sign – a message, if you will – that you really are chipping away at the problem.

I know that struggling on when you feel you have had enough is extremely hard. But try to see progress as the underlying message and fight the temptation to give up – however strong it is.

Preparing for these problems in advance may help you feel ready for any challenges when they crop up.

Resolutions exercise

Can you recall if there were certain feelings or circumstances that made you give up on a new resolution (such as following a diet or an exercise programme, or deciding to watch less television)? Jot down the event and, if you can, the feelings that led to your losing your resolve. If you parent with a partner, try doing this exercise together.

✎ . . . .

. . . .

. . . .

. . . .

. . . .

. . . .

. . . .

. . . .

. . . .

. . . .

. . . .

. . . .

. . . .

. . . .

. . . .

. . . .

Study what you have written. You have experienced these feelings time and time again. They form your personal response to uphill struggles – watch out for them creeping in as you progress through ADDapt.

CHAPTER 8

Be Consistent

Golden Rule No. 4: Be consistent

Be consistent in what you say and do. Be consistent in the way you apply ADDapt. Be consistent with your co-parents – work as a united team.

Inconsistency and ADD

For all parents, being consistent all the time in the way we treat our children is one of the hardest things to do. Let's face it, there are times when we all lose the plot in our parenting and fail to be consistent. For example:

- We lose our temper and end up forgetting what we were telling the child to do.

- We give commands that we do not follow up.

- We make threats like 'Do that once more and you'll go to bed!', or 'That's it, I'm telling Daddy when he comes home', and then do nothing.

ADD children are particularly sensitive to inconsistency. They find mixed messages confusing. They may test you out in challenging ways just to establish what you mean by the contradictory things you say and do. Being consistent is your main tool for remedying this.

1. Be consistent in what you say and do

Remember that all young children, and especially children with ADD, tend to take what we say literally. As adults we often don't expect to be taken literally. An extravagant threat, like the ones above, may be just an expression of our anger or frustration.

An ADD child will not recognise this. He or she will be confused if you don't follow through. And the same goes for rewards and praising. Once you start a positive change you need to keep it up.

The best policy is: don't make threats, give promises or embark on tasks you are not prepared to carry through to the end.

2. Be consistent in the way you apply ADDapt

Because consistency is so important, I recommend that you fight the temptation to try other strategies or techniques that have been recommended by a friend or relative at the same time as using the ideas in this book. I'm not saying that I have all the answers or that nobody has equally good ideas. What I am suggesting is – just try one thing at a time. If you don't, your child may become hopelessly bewildered and you may be back to square one.

3. Be consistent with each other

ADDapt works equally well for single parents and for couples (and for anyone else in a parental role). However, I need to stress that where two or more people share the parenting, it is vital that you are all consistent with each other in what you say and do, always adopting the same strategies and backing each other up.

The ADDapt Programme

Keeping on Task
Powerful Motivators

Congratulations, you have got this far! Give yourself a pat on the back. Let's start on the programme. Step 1 is about *you* and will help you prepare for the tasks ahead. Whenever your resolve begins to falter come back to this chapter to refresh your stamina. In Step 1 you will:

- learn how to develop your own powerful motivators – the ones that work best for you

- learn new techniques to empower yourself any time you need to.

I will give you:

- specific directions on what to do

- tips for avoiding pitfalls

- tips for getting off to a positive start.

Motivators: Our natural defences

What are 'motivators'? Motivators are messages inside our heads that tell us, 'Basically, you're all right. Things are going OK. We're doing the best we can. You're not going to give up because...' Beliefs like these function rather like an emotional immune system to keep our morale up and our resolve strong. They provide us with the drive and energy to apply ourselves to things we believe in. They are mental catch-phrases or slogans that sum up what is important in our lives and in the lives of those close to us. Therapists call them 'anchors' because they anchor the emotion and energy you need to the phrase or idea. Our ability to keep a balance between the frustrations and pleasures in life may well depend on these natural defences against negativity and self-doubt.

Beware demotivators

Powerful demotivators have the opposite effect on you. They make your energy and resolve drain away. These negative beliefs sap your resolve by telling you, 'You will fail' or 'You haven't got what it takes' or 'Why did this have to happen to you?' Once they get a hold upon you, these ways of seeing yourself can make you less productive. They don't serve any useful purpose and are in fact terribly unhelpful.

Boost your motivation system

Your faith in ADDapt may falter when you have setbacks. At such times you need to remind yourself of the beliefs that got you started in the first place and have carried you as far as you have got.

You can train your brain to get into gear by reminding yourself of the goals you have and the reasons for them. This is what motivators do. Thoughts such as 'I'll do anything for my child', 'I always put my children first', 'I put their happiness at the top of the list' spur you on to make an effort when your spirit is sagging. The bottom line is that there are motivators that are right for you. Finding them is a personal thing. What motivates some will only upset others, but in general, messages based on achieving good things are better than messages based on avoiding bad things. Here are some basic ideas of how to go about it. First, identify statements that highlight positives:

- about yourself
- about your child
- about your relationship or the good times you have together.

Then try to capture the essence of those thoughts in a phrase or slogan that has significance for you. Here are some examples:

Potential motivators	Watch out for potential demotivators
About yourself: 'I've always given 110% to my kids.' 'If something blocks me I go round it.' 'I'm a trier.' 'I'm a survivor.' 'Once I can see where I'm going, I know I will get there somehow.'	'No one else will care if I don't.' 'I'm all she's got left.' 'We'll see, but...' 'I can't feel any lower, so I can only feel better.'
About your child: 'He'll show them all, one day.' 'He'll give his last penny to anyone.' 'He can't do enough for me when I'm ill.' 'He never gives up and always bounces back.'	'He's got his good points – if you look **hard** for them.' 'He can be an angel – if he **wants** to be'. 'He'll do anything for **others**.' 'He'll do what he **wants** to do.'
About your relationship: 'He always gives me a cuddle when I need it.' 'He gives the best hugs in the world.' 'I remember...he was so great that day – I was so proud.'	'We're stuck with each other.' 'I can't send him back, can I!' 'It's too hard to think of good times.'

The key to building up positive resources in your parenting lies in finding powerful motivators that work for you and using them often, revising them and making up new ones as you go. The exercise that follows encourages you to take the time to find out what motivates you.

Motivators exercise

Write down three powerful motivators – three ideas that you are absolutely committed to and that will drive you to carry on when the going gets tough.

1. . . . .

2. . . . .

3. . . . .

Now, on your own, where no one can overhear you, say your motivators out loud. Put feeling and emotion into the words and feel the power of the words inside you. Once you have repeated them a few times, stop saying them out loud and start saying them inside your head. I know that this may feel silly, but it works. It works because you are *anchoring*, or fixing, these beliefs into your mind and you are reinforcing them by generating the emotion they produce within you. Do this anchoring exercise, and these new beliefs will become part of how you think. Call on your motivators as often as you like; at least daily at first, and then whenever you feel you need a boost. Here is another exercise to boost your positive feelings as you begin Step 2:

Building-the-positives exercise

The positive and loving feelings that you have for your child are always there, but at times of stress they slip beneath the surface. This
exercise gets you to focus on these positive feelings and how much
they mean to you. On your own, take a pen and a pad or write below the thoughts that come into your mind in answering the following questions:

• What things are great and unique about my child?

• When I think about her, what do I feel grateful for?

• What are all the things I love and value about her personality?

While you are writing, pause occasionally, and just reflect on how
you feel when you think of your child in this way.

   You can use the power of these emotions to motivate yourself to
create changes in both you and your child. It's also a good way of
making contact with those all-important motivating phrases or
statements that we just covered.

Who's the Boss? 'Special Time'

A New Approach

Welcome to Step 2. Let's get started on the relationship between you and your child.

You want her behaviour to change. The way you are handling it is not achieving your goal. Agreed? When you try to change your child you try to control her behaviour in some way. You become the boss! All parents have to struggle with control when relating to their child. Since you are the parent of a child with ADD, you will struggle more than most. Control in a relationship can have some very negative side-effects. It can drive a parent and child apart. You will hear more about this in a moment.

Step 2 gives you a fresh approach to this whole issue. It is based on improving the understanding between you and your child. It will be fun. You will enjoy it and so will your child.

During Step 2 you will:

- set up regular 'play times' with your child which will make her more cooperative

- learn to avoid escalating rows where you and your child are angry or aggressive with each other

- anticipate problems in advance and feel ready for those challenges when they crop up.

The issue of control

ADD children are different when it comes to doing as they are told. Most children dislike being told what to do, but ADD children tend to show their displeasure in intense and extreme ways. They learn the skills of self-control and compliance more slowly. They often resort to severe tantrums and explosive outbursts when they can't get their own way. This comes from the hyperactive and impulsive aspects of their condition. If the question of who gets his or her way is a frequent source of conflict between you and your ADD child, then you need to create more times when the issue of control is absent. A holiday from the struggle for control is what Special Time is all about.

Julie and Molly

Julie is a single parent with a five-year-old daughter, Molly. Molly was diagnosed as having ADD a year ago. She has been prescribed 20ml Ritalin a day, which has improved her ability to listen and pay attention to what is said to her. As a result, her reading and writing skills are better and she is doing more chores around the house. But tantrums are still common. The following row between Julie and her daughter shows how bad things were getting before she started the programme:

Julie and Molly continued

Julie has daily rows with Molly at breakfast. Today she asks Molly to put her cup in the sink before she plays in the garden. Molly says no. Julie raises her voice: 'Put it in the sink.' Molly screams at the top of her voice, 'NOOOOOOOO!' Julie has been here many times before, but she is shocked by the volume and the aggression in her daughter's voice. She is stunned into silence. Molly stomps by her into the garden. Julie tells herself, 'Forget it ... Anything for a quiet life' (not exactly the most inspiring motivator!). She lets it go.

Five minutes later Molly is banging hard on the window: 'I want a biscuit.' Julie feels Molly has already had her own way about the cup, and decides 'no biscuit'. She ignores Molly's banging. Soon it grows louder and louder. In a rage Julie flies out of the door, grabs Molly by the arm, marches her to the kitchen, points at the cup and shrieks, 'Put it in the sink now! You stupid, horrible girl!'

Molly breaks from her mother's grip, screams, 'I hate you!' and throws the cup on the floor – it smashes – then runs from the house into the garden.

Julie is furious. She thinks: 'She's running my life. **Like she's the boss.**'

But she doesn't chase after her daughter. She knows that if she catches her this morning she will hit Molly and won't be able to stop. Anyway, she cannot face another row. So Molly runs into the garden. Julie calms herself down – this may take 10 or 15 minutes. But the resentment goes much deeper. All day Julie feels 'I really hate her. I know I shouldn't but sometimes I do.'

On the surface it might look as if Molly has won this battle. In fact, both mother *and* child have been the losers. The anger that smoulders inside Julie lasts for three days and, as Julie told me, 'It affects how we relate to each other. When I feel like this I don't want to get close to her.' Clearly, there is a growing distance between them. Molly will pick up these feelings – all children do – and in turn feel angry and insecure. The chances are that if Julie and Molly find themselves in a similar situation tomorrow another 'battle' will ensue. This time Julie may appear to win. Or maybe Molly. Whoever 'wins', their feelings towards each other are growing more confused and angry.

So is the answer more of the same?

You might be thinking, 'Why doesn't this woman just put her foot down and put an end to all the tension that is building up between them?' Well, Julie would be the first to admit that she may not have been as firm or consistent as she could have been with Molly in the past. But the questions now are: *Should Julie continue to concentrate on who is being the boss?* and *Is more discipline the answer at this stage?* In my view the answer is 'no'. If your ADD child acts as Molly does, then banging away at 'Who's the boss?' can often turn out to be at the cost of your relationship.

What is really needed at this point is more time when the issue of control is absent from the interaction between mother and child – not better ways for Julie to get control over Molly. This is where Special Time comes in.

Special Time for young children

Special Time is a unique play time shared by one parent and one child. Special Time is about setting up short periods during the day (say, twice a day) when positive feelings can flow. It is useful for all children between the ages of two and seven. (For older children, Special Time requires some adaptation to reflect their more mature interests and ways of playing. See Appendix 2, but read this section too for the general principles.)

Play is one of the most important ways that children learn. Therefore play time is one of the best times to influence how a child behaves.

During play, children try out things that they have seen adults do, develop their own personality and evolve ways of communicating with others. For most children it is a happy and positive time. And playing together in the absence of control, correction and coercion can be fun! It also changes patterns in your relationship – in three important ways:

1. Letting your child take the lead when you play together gives both of you an experience of him or her being in control and taking responsibility in a context he or she enjoys. You are free to play too, because you don't have to be in charge.

2. It frees you to observe just how amazing your child's imagination and creativity can be.

3. By providing you both with a breathing space to play together, Special Time reminds you of the warmth and enjoyment that you can get from each other. These feelings often evaporate when you fight over who is boss.

Because Special Time is a boss-free zone you can build mutual understanding without conflict.

SUMMARY: HOW SPECIAL TIME WORKS

- Children associate play with fun and positive feelings.

- You give positive attention to your child, which builds affection and trust.

- You both get conflict-free time during each day.

- Your child takes the lead, so there are no battles over who's the boss.

- New techniques promote better understanding between you.

- You influence each other by getting closer.

Setting up Special Time

Pick two occasions during a normal day when you can spend 10–15 minutes with your child. At the beginning the other children – if you have any – are not included in the Special Time with your ADD child.

As far as you can, make this a regular slot. It doesn't necessarily mean the same time every day (though a routine certainly helps with ADD kids), but it does mean it should happen each day if at all possible.

This is the kind of thing you might say to your child to get things started: 'Molly, you remember I said we were arguing a lot – well, Mummy wants some time to play with you and we won't get cross with each other. Show me a game we could do together.' Simple. You don't need to give any more rules than that at this stage.

Since the aim of Special Time is to give your child an opportunity to take the lead in a game or a task you do together, *your role is to follow.* The best way to show that you are following is through what you say and do. Positive-attention skills help you to do this.

Positive-attention skills

To follow your child effectively you must let her know that you are observing closely what she is doing and what she is saying. In the jargon this skill is called 'attending positively'. It means responding actively to your child, making frequent comments to show how closely you are observing and listening to what she is doing and saying. The message you want give to her is 'I am really interested in you.' The aim in learning these skills is always to be and to sound as natural as possible.

Here are some examples of Julie giving Molly some positive attention as she plays in a sandpit during Special Time:

'Gosh! You have made a really weird shape there.'

'You're going to have a humungous hole in a minute.'

'What an amazing jump! And another one.'

'Molly, you love sand so much.'

This might sound a bit odd or artificial at first. But it will become more natural as time goes on. This approach is *attentive* because you are giving feedback all the time that you are watching and listening to your child, and *positive* because it is promoting behaviour in her that you can feel positive about and give praise for.

Develop positive-attention skills during Special Time

Things to avoid	Bad habits	Try instead
Don't be teacher – don't turn the game or task into a lesson	'The digger is purple, Molly not blue. Can you spell purple? C'mon – after me , P.U.R.P.L.E. C'mon.' 'OK, that's how many shells? C'mon – four plus seven is?'	'You've made a massive castle with that digger.' 'You're putting the shells into groups. That's good.'
Don't correct.	'Look at your painting…you don't get red skies, do you?' 'Can't you stick to the paper not the table when you're colouring in!'	Let her keep the sky red if that's what she has done. 'What a lovely red your sky is.'
Don't point out how to do it better.	'No, no, you'll never make pastry with all that water…watch what I'm doing.'	'Molly's pastry is going to have loads of water in it.'
Don't criticise.	'No. That's not right, is it!'	Focus on the positives.

Cut down the questions

This is hard to do. You'd be amazed how much of parents' interactions with children are based on questions. Asking questions means that *you control the conversation, not them.* As an experiment, try not asking questions for five minutes while playing with your child. Hard, isn't it! For a change, get into the practice of swapping questions for statements during Special Time.

Swap questions for statements

	Avoid saying		Try instead
✗	'What are you going to do with all that sand?'	✓	'The sand is really piling up.'
✗	'What are you doing with those bricks?'	✓	'Molly, the bricks are being buried.'
✗	'What are you going to do with those shells?'	✓	'Molly's sorting the shells out.'
✗	'Where are you putting the water?'	✓	'That looks as if it might be a moat.'

Cut out all commands!

For example:

✗   'This way!'

✗   'Do it like this!'

✗   'Don't do that!'

Now get into practice

Special Time works – trust me on this. At first it can seem a lot of effort in order to produce small changes, but the changes will get bigger as time moves on. It is crucial to practise Special Time regularly, especially at the start. It's the frequency that ensures faster progress. Try to practise Special Time at least once a day, for 10–15 minutes.

After each Special Time, complete the check-list on page 63 to judge how things are proceeding.

If you react strongly against the idea of Special Time, can I suggest that you reread Chapters 6, 7 and 8 again? How's that for bossiness!

Frequently asked questions

Q: *'How can I find the time?'*

A: This is the commonest question I am asked about Special Time, and one I have no easy answer to. If you have worries about making enough time, you are not alone. The lives of parents today are busier than ever, and with extended family often living far away, support can be hard to find. Other parents have told me of just this kind of difficulty – for example: 'I felt mean not giving my older son Special Time too, so I've started it for both of them, which has cut out any jealousy but it really eats up my time', 'I'm a single parent with another, younger, child, and getting regular help to practise Special Time isn't easy', and 'My wife and I both do shift work … one of us going out when the other comes in … we needed to be so organised to find out who had done what around play times.'

There is no magic solution to shortage of time. All I can do is to keep reminding you that making the time for Special Time could be one of the best investments you'll ever make.

Q: *'How long does it take?'*

A: I am asking you to try it regularly for three months. After two months most parents can see a dramatic improvement that others will notice and remark on. Within six months the necessity for regular sessions will have gone. By this time positive-attention skills will be part of your daily interactions with your child. Reach this point, and your relationship with him will have changed for ever.

Q: *'What if we miss a practice?'*

A: Six or seven sessions a week will start to produce a noticeable change in your relationship within two weeks. Three or four sessions a week will mean change is much slower. One or two sessions a week will probably produce little or no change.

Q: *'How can special time help me when it's naughty behaviour that is such a problem?'*

A: Special Time sneaks up on naughty behaviour. Being naughty has become one of the ways your child has learned to get your attention. Special Time shows him how to get your attention by being good.

ADD children and their parents often find themselves shouting and screaming at each other. Sometimes these angry feelings mean that you and your child have grown apart in small ways. You may find that you are constantly not relaxed, on the alert for naughty behaviour. You may happen to miss the times when your child is being good and so he may think that the best way to grab your attention is by being naughty. The Special Time will remind you how much you love each other and will make it easier for you to be positive.

Q: *'Are you suggesting that we don't love each other?'*

A: No. But many parents have told us that Special Time helped them to realise that they had not spent as much quality time with their child as they wanted to because the angry times had taken over.

Q: *'Can you say more about the idea behind letting the child take the lead?'*

A: As adults, we get used to taking charge of our children because they need us to protect and take care of them. But it is normal for children to want independence and to want to feel in charge of themselves. Special Time is a good way for you to encourage this aspect of your child's development. Special Time has been designed to encourage your skills in allowing your child a chance to take the lead in a positive way.

Q: *'When should we have Special Time?'*

A: The rule has to be: Better at any time than not at all. But always remember that ADD kids respond best to consistency. They easily forget tasks that don't fall into a routine. You will probably find it easier to organise Special Time if it forms part of a daily routine that your child can get used to. A set routine is not essential, but it may be very helpful in reducing protest and conflict between you.

A suggestion one parent found effective was to draw a clock face on a big sheet of paper next to the kitchen clock. When the time arrived she would simply announce, 'It's our Special Time, what should we do?' Try it. Your child may have something in mind – if not, wait and see what develops.

Q: *'What if he does not want to do anything with me?'*

A: Special Time should not be a chore for either of you, but a space where you can have fun together. 'I don't want to play with you' should be accepted by you without protest. Stay calm. Be as open and friendly as possible during the time you have set aside. Simply say that you would like to use the Special Time together anyway. If you feel comfortable, carry on playing on your own and you may find your child comes to join you. Most children cannot resist the invitation to play, and pretty soon will want to get in on the act!

If you still have a problem, ask yourself, 'How good am I at getting fun times to happen?' Try thinking of three ways that you could get a game started if your child seems uninterested.

Q: 'Should I push him into the Special Time?'

A: No. Sometimes your child may be in a mood with you, and show little interest in play. Don't be put off. Make use of any sign that he would rather play than sulk. Once he begins to get the idea he will want more of your positive attention and praise and will do more to please you.

Q: 'My son is naughty during Special Time. Should I end it?'

A: Yes and no. Always ignore his naughty behaviour unless something or someone is going to get damaged. If that happens, simply say, 'we cannot carry on while you are doing that. Do you want to play or stop?' If he stops immediately and wants to play properly it is right to let the game carry on, but if the same dangerous behaviour recurs, time together must stop. This may create a little bit of bad feeling, so look for an opportunity to offer some praise to your child so as to lighten the tension that may now exist.

TIP FOR SUCCESS

- The key to good Special Time is *trying it!* You can analyse it if you want, or criticise it if you want, but these might be delaying tactics. So do something different – *try it.*

Check out your positive-attention skills

Tick as appropriate, and see how you score.

Task	Very often	Often	Hardly ever
How many times did you describe what your child was doing? e.g. 'You're building a tower.'			
How often did you describe what she was playing with? e.g. 'That's a red brick.' 'That's a green car.'			
How many times did you join in her play? e.g. Your child: 'I'm going to bury you alive.' you: 'I'm going to turn into a zombie.'			
Have you praised her?			
Were you able to ignore or distract her from naughty attention-seeking behaviour?			
Did you manage to **avoid**			
1. telling her what to do?			
2. asking her too many questions?			
3. criticising or pointing out how to improve?			

The Home Points System

Part 1

By this stage Special Time should be well under way and will have become part of your daily schedule. Although there may have been (perhaps still are) some teething problems, you are probably already noticing the benefits of greater closeness. Now I want to reinforce the positive message that your child is receiving from you. I am asking you to set up a reward system that demonstrates that you are noticing, every day, what your child is doing right.

In this Step you will:

- learn how to set up a Home Points System

- become expert in giving other incentives, in addition to praise

- chart your child's achievements daily.

How does the Home Points System (or HPS) work?

Home Points Systems are sometimes called 'token economies'. This is because, in the past, plastic tokens were given in exchange for good behaviour. 'Economy' is an appropriate word, because you are setting up a simple barter system which states that if a child behaves in a certain way, his parents will provide rewards and/or privileges in return.

This is how the system works. You, the parents, 'pay out' points to your child, who earns them by conforming to simple rules and appropriate behaviour. Points earned can be 'cashed in' for rewards each day or saved up for a bigger prize. The whole project is agreed to by everyone – especially the child – like a contract.

Why does it work so well with ADD kids?

1. It provides concrete incentives.

2. It structures expectations from parents.

3. It makes the HPS – not you – the Big Bad Boss!

The HPS sounds simple, but it can be hard to put into practice effectively. You may have already tried something similar – a star chart, for instance. But you may also have found it didn't work. Other books and professionals who recommend them often skip over the finer details – details that are central to success or failure.

NOTE

What follows has been written with a child of six years plus in mind. If your child is between four and six you will need to consult the special guidelines on page 72 as well. HPSs do not work well for children under four.

Setting up the HPS

There are two key actions that you need to undertake. With each key action you will be given Tips for Success, which are your essential guide to overcoming the pitfalls at each stage. Read them carefully.

Key action 1 – List 'more-ofs'

'More-of' behaviours are those that you expect your child to exhibit more frequently or that do not occur now. On a sheet of paper, prepare a list of behaviours that you want to see more of from him or her.

Be sure to include only those behaviours that you are certain he or she is capable of, if properly motivated. For example, 'Sort your life out' might be a tall order for the best of us; it's also very vague. So keep your targets crystal-clear and doable. Exhortations like 'Be more cooperative' or 'Have a good attitude' are out! Replace them with 'Say good morning to Dad and Mum.' It will be clear whether it has been done or not.

More-of behaviours

1. Be out of bed by 7.30 a.m.

2. Load the dishwasher once a week

3. Brush teeth morning and night

4. Start homework at 5 p.m.

5. ✎

See the chart below and draw one like it, filling in the more-ofs from your list.

I want to see more of these	Points each is worth	Points that you have earned						
		Mon	Tues	Weds	Thurs	Fri	Sat	Sun
Out of bed by 7.30a.m.	10 per day	-						
Load the dishwasher	30 per week	30						
Brush teeth morning and night	10 per day	10						
Extra credit		5						
Total points		45						

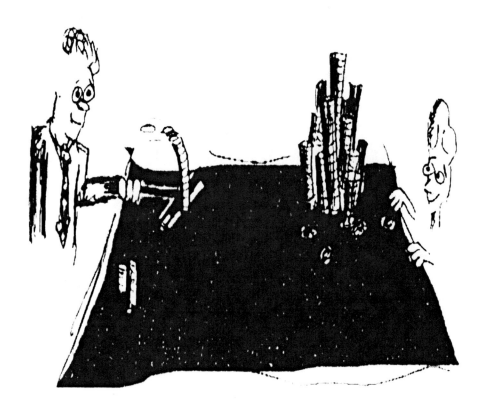

Look who's winning!

You will notice that there is an additional line called 'extra credit'. You can use this to enable your child to earn extra points for displaying behaviour not on the list but which you are especially pleased with.

TIPS FOR SUCCESS

- Setting the right number of points is important. The value needs to be high enough to encourage your child to have a go. Always give a higher value to behaviour that you value more. For instance, completing half an hour's homework is usually worth more than emptying the bin.

- Give frequent rewards. For those more-of behaviours that you want to happen several times a day at appropriate times, such as 'Brush your teeth' or 'Say please and thank-you', pick a maximum number of times that you will reward them each day. Put these numbers in brackets on the chart. This should avoid having your child say 'please' every two seconds or brush his teeth away so as to get a hundred points.

BEFORE YOU GO ON ...

Check once again that your targets are:

1. Do-able

2. Crystal-clear

Key action 2 – list the rewards

On a sheet of paper, list a number of rewards or privileges that your child could spend the points on.

Rewards

1. Extra hour of TV

2. Having a sleep-over

3. Picking the video game

4. Staying up for 'Match of the Day' on Saturday

5. Having a friend over on ✎

Now, draw up a new chart like the one below.

Rewards	Points each costs	Points that you have spent						
		Mon	Tues	Weds	Thurs	Fri	Sat	Sun
Staying up for 'Match of the Day'	50	-						
Extra hour of TV	20	-						
Picking the video game	180	-						
No chores to do for today	20	20						
Total points		20						

It's good practice to include at least seven rewards and privileges on the chart, so that your child has some choice over how to spend the points.

Once you have listed the rewards and privileges on offer, assign a points value to each one. But be careful. This can be tricky. The rule is: the cost should be low enough to give the child an opportunity to earn a reward or two each day, yet high enough that the privileges are not earned too easily. If your child is earning a lot of points, it's usually a sign that the programme is working well. Especially in the early stages, don't be reluctant to:

- give your child points

- point out when he does well

- offer extra credits.

Stick your charts to the kitchen wall. Now you have a Home Points System that you can use to get you started. It is based on positive goals and rewards only. At this stage *no* points are taken away.

MORE TIPS FOR SUCCESS

- Spend, spend, spend! Bear in mind this is not the harsh reality of a business economy. You want your child to participate and to succeed: *so be generous.* Being too tough or stingy can wreck your chances – particularly in the early stages.

- Avoid having a list full of privileges that can only be paid for once a month. It is crucial that your list should contain rewards and privileges that the child can spend her points on at least once a day. ADD children often need easy wins when they are trying to change. To begin with, it is important to see that your child gets the regular reinforcement of a treat earned each day. If she has a bad day points can dry up and the big prize – e.g. a video recorder at 2000 points – may drift away from her. It is much better to offer rewards such as half an hour's TV (for 50 points), which can be earned and spent daily, than a big 1000-point prize that may never materialise.

- Don't deduct points for bad behaviour – 'less-of' behaviours are coming, but don't jump the gun. Your child must first earn some points and get some rewards. If you start deducting points too early she will not earn the numbers of points that make rewards and privileges possible. Often a child will acquire minus points within a few days. This only lowers her self-confidence and frightens her off the HPS.

- A positive start is crucial – introduce the programme to your child in a positive manner. Explain that you have learned a method by which she may be able to earn rewards and privileges by being good. Be creative with younger children, who can get really excited by the idea of a game. Spark their imagination!

- Involve your child. It is very important that she has time to understand what you are trying to do. Remember, you must review the rewards and privilege list with her, and try to establish incentives that appeal to her. Explain the behaviours that you want to see more of. Let her know why you have put them on the list. Explain their value in points and tell her the positive change that your joint efforts will bring to both your life and hers.

- Review! Review! Having done all this, it's usually wise to go back over the rewards and privileges with your child to see if she has got any extra suggestions about the cost of each privilege and the types of reward that you have selected.

Frequently asked questions

Q: *'Will it work?'*

A: Yes, in almost all cases, if you follow the rules.

Q: *'What if my child hoards points?'*

A: *Warning*: Hoarder! Children often hoard points to earn something they really prize. Some can only be motivated by a larger reward. If you have a hoarder on your hands, there is no point in fighting against it. Let your child accumulate points. The trick is to keep the value of the prize she has set her heart on relatively low. If it is too high she is liable to miss out and become disappointed, with the added danger that she may turn against the HPS. This you *don't* want.

Q: *'Should I include my other children in the HPS?'*

A: Why not? In my experience most children benefit from the structure and incentives offered by the system. There's a chance that your ADD child will feel less as if she has been singled out if you do.

Q: *'Is my child too young to understand an HPS – particularly the points and totals?'*

A: Good point. For younger children some special guidelines apply.

TIPS FOR SUCCESS WITH YOUNGER CHILDREN

- Use little drawings to depict the more-of behaviours. A match-stick figure getting out of bed or putting clothes on is fine to show this is one of the behaviours you are looking for.

- But keep up the writing too – it helps their learning.

- Numbers are often too abstract for younger children. Things that can be seen and touched have more meaning, so convert points into plastic tokens. Have a jar ready to collect these – and make it visible.

- Don't make your token system too elaborate. Some parents opt for different-coloured tokens, others use plastic money – the majority rely on a simple system to ensure that their four- or five-year-old can follow what is going on.

- 'Star charts' are becoming popular in many primary schools. Copy the same system at home if your child is on one at school. This may be less confusing than having two different systems.

- With younger children, make the most of the ritual of giving and spending tokens. Counting them out, putting them into the jar and taking them out to spend should be 'played up' to ensure it holds their interest.

- Keep reinforcing the principles of the HPS as you go along: 'Brushed your teeth today…no fuss…two red ones. Well done.' 'Very good boy at Granny's today…there was no fighting or arguing…five extra tokens.'

    'Want to spend some tokens tonight?… You've got plenty – you've been very good lately.'

- If your child still doesn't get the point of the chart at this stage, the best system is the most basic – tokens as rewards for things he does right, collected in a jar and spent on a treat when you visit the shops. Don't forget, even with a basic system it is crucial to encourage regular spending.

NOTE

Do not start this part of the programme if you or your child are confused. This will mean you will run into difficulties early on and may give up through lack of success.

Praise – Your Secret Weapon

Welcome back! You have been very busy. Special Time will be very familiar to you by now. Also, you have set up the HPS and are recording and rewarding your child daily. Well done – you really are doing a great job.

By the way, if you are remortgaging your home to fund the rewards you give on the HPS, you've taken a wrong turn! Remember, small rewards that don't cost money are the key, even in today's materialistic world.

If, at times, you have been really cross with your child over the last few weeks and have been tempted to deduct points, *don't*. Trust me, that moment will come, but now is definitely not the time.

You may have noticed that since you have been using Special Time there has been a tendency for your child to behave better when he has you all to himself and worse when having to share your attention. This is common. Don't worry at this stage. I'm sure you are still getting tantrums and defiance, but we are only at Step 4. Change will almost certainly take longer to became apparent.

The next three steps take you through the skills you need in order to tackle all the forms of attention-seeking that your child presents you with. The first skill is praise. You will learn how to do it effectively and how powerful it can be.

Some facts about praise

Praise is one of the most effective ways of helping children change, and one of the most neglected. Given clearly and often, praise is your secret weapon against the worst aspects of ADD behaviour:

- aggression
- defiance
- stubbornness
- fighting

- tantrums
- swearing
- arguing back
- spitefulness

I tell you this because I want you to know that over time the *brashest, most in-your-face children* have been won over by praise. Believe me, I have seen it.

The hidden cost of criticism

For many ADD children life offers a monotonous diet of reprimands, criticism and punishment from teachers, classmates and those they love and depend on. ADD kids know only too well that the things they do frustrate, annoy – *enrage* – others. What they know too little of is what they do that pleases, excites and thrills. No wonder they have low self-esteem.

Defiance, the 'don't give a damn' attitude, aggression, dumb insolence and many other behaviours that set ADD kids apart may in fact be a mask for feelings such as:

- being desperate to please someone
- crying out for approval
- feeling insecure and unsure of their self-worth
- feeling hungry for praise
- poor self-image
- lack of confidence.

These are feelings that are particularly hard for children to put into words.

Praise is valuable to your child

ADD children thrive on attention and develop better when the attention is positive. Praise brings out the best in them – as it does with all of us. But praise works especially for ADD kids because it shows that someone has taken the time to spot their value, their efforts or their qualities. Sadly, for parents coping with the stress of ADD praise can become as forgotten as vinyl records.

In my experience, the more you pile praise on an ADD child the more he realises that he *can* actually please you. His condition makes him forgetful and easily distracted, so he needs frequent reminders of this. It means catching your child doing something right and making sure you are organising things so that he can do something right as often as possible. If all you do is point out things he does wrong, you steadily chip away at his self-esteem.

Reward good behaviour

The central message couldn't be simpler: to show your child he can please you by being good, you must **praise, praise and praise again**. The key to transformation is *persistence* on your part and coming up with *variety* in the ways you give praise.

From now on, always be on the lookout for anything good about your child's behaviour and reward it with attention and praise. No matter how small a thing it is, note it and praise it. From now on, if he does something good like dressing himself without being told, show him you have seen it and show him that you appreciate it. Don't just take it for granted because he should have done it anyway. Always praise any behaviour you want to see more of.

Spotting-success exercise

Ask yourself: 'Are there three things that I can think of that my child is already doing well? Am I praising him for what he has achieved?'

1. . . . .

2. . . . .

3. . . . .

Awash-with-praise exercise

Ask yourself: 'What else can I praise him for and encourage him to do more often?'

1. . . . .

2. . . . .

3. . . . .

Build self-esteem

Once your child is used to receiving praise for things that he already does, look for opportunities to praise and encourage him in new areas.

Notice him being more self-reliant, more independent, and reward it immediately with praise – instances such as:

- Not interrupting when you and your partner are having a conversation. Turn to your child and say, 'Well done, Tommy – you didn't interrupt. That's much better.'

- Playing with a puzzle for two or three minutes – 'That's good, Tommy, you're playing nicely.'

- Not shouting at the top of his voice – 'Hey, that's great, Tommy. You can be so quiet.'

And so on. The more the better.

Moments like these currently occur far less than you want. All the more reason to offer praise *the instant* they happen. Hearing warm words from you at these moments will be unexpected. It will build your child's self-esteem and self-worth.

In fact, feel free to go over the top. Get really excited about the slightest thing he does right. Really build him up. It doesn't matter if he thinks you're going crazy – it's only because he has never been used to this much praise. And it doesn't matter if everyone else thinks you're crazy too. *They* should have to cope with what you have to deal with every day!

TIPS FOR SUCCESS

- Praise instantly. ADD kids forget quickly and need instant gratification.

- *Never say nothing* on the assumption that your child *knows* you are pleased.

- Be as specific as possible. Being specific tells your child how to please you and what it is that has generated your praise. Never assume that he understands exactly what has given rise to the praise. For example, 'Good boy for saying thank-you', 'That's good, it really pleases me when you're polite like that' are better than the nonspecific 'Well done', 'Clever lad'.

- Try to set up opportunities for *overheard praise*, when your child can hear you talking positively about him to someone else. For example, when on the phone to Granny or Dad and in earshot of your child, say something like 'He was really good today – he tidied his room, really set an example to Ronnie and his friends.'
  If someone calls round, make a point of getting him to 'overhear' you reporting how well he is doing (even if there is little to report, bend the truth a little). *Children will live up to a good reputation as readily as they will live up to a bad one.*

- Praise often – you cannot praise too much, and there is always something else you can notice to praise.
  There appears to be a myth – probably dating from the 1940s – that if you praise a child too much you will produce a cocky, precocious individual. The result has been that British parents, in particular, have held back overt expressions of approval and praise. But there can be no doubt that the best way to raise a child to become emotionally secure, to have high self-esteem and to be generous to others in later life is to praise him and tell him how fantastic he is, throughout childhood.

- *Immediate praise is more valuable than the promise of future rewards.* I am not a great believer in the delayed-gratification approach, by which I mean saying things like 'Keep up the good behaviour and *we'll see* what you get on Saturday.' Working towards a larger reward, which takes time to earn, *can* work, but ADD kids sometimes stumble along the way. If their hope for a treat is dashed because they took one step forward and two back, they will feel disappointed, even despairing. These feelings get expressed as anger, which will drive parent and child apart. Remember that for children, a big treat as a way of saying 'Well done' is much more exciting, and therefore more effective, when it comes as a surprise.

- Be spontaneous – Just do it.

Frequently asked questions

Q: *'Aren't you saying I should praise him for what he* should *be doing, but isn't?'*

A: Absolutely. He's *not* doing it, and praising him stands a good chance of making it happen.

Q: *'I seem to be doing all the giving, becoming a complete softie.'*

A: ADDapt is designed this way. I have 'softened you up' for a purpose. Problems arise in ADD children because they learn the three Cs of confrontation, criticism and control too early. By focusing on the three As of acceptance, anticipation and approval I hope to have increased the emotional connectedness between you and your child.

Q: *'What about the other kids – won't they feel all these verbal rewards show favouritism?'*

A: So what? Tell them you love them just as much, but you are trying to improve things for their brother or sister. If it is not too complicated and they are old enough, why not recruit them to help you in offering positives to their sibling?

RECAP

- Task 1 – praise whatever your child is currently doing well.

- Task 2 – praise whatever you want to see more of.

FINAL TIP FOR SUCCESS

- Perhaps you are missing some opportunities for praise! Remember
  what the American writer Dale Carnegie wrote in his book *How to
  Win Friends and Influence People*: 'Flattery works even when people
  know you're doing it' (1930). Do not worry that too much praise
  could be counterproductive. Making a child feel better about
  himself through praise has no drawbacks whatsoever.

NOTE

It really enforces your ability to praise and encourage your child if you can
surround *yourself* with praise and encouragement. Getting your partner, friend or
relative to read this chapter might galvanise him or her into showering you with
praise and support. We all have the knack of pointing out what others could do
better! As a parent with an ADD child, you need loved ones to back you up. They
can do this by employing the techniques in this chapter – spotting what *you* are
doing right, praising you for it and repeating it until you believe it. See also
Appendix 1, 'Working in Partnership'.

Tackling Attention-Seeking

To make your child's behaviour change you need to master three communication skills over all others:

1. praising so as to boost self-esteem (Step 4): You have made this first step and you are praising like mad...so here's some more from me – well done!

2. ignoring negative attention-seeking (Step 5)

3. giving clear commands (Step 6).

Step 5 shows the powerful ignoring strategies you need so as to eliminate from your lives the dominance of tantrums, whingeing and endless demanding. Ignoring 'silliness' is as important as praise, but it can be a lot more difficult.

In Step 5 you will learn:

- why children with ADD are hooked on attention-seeking

- what to ignore

- how to ignore it.

Your only new task is to read the section below and undertake the exercise at the end.

Your next big challenge

Along with praising good behaviour, ignoring attention-seeking is your next big task. We all know what we're talking about here. An ADD child will tend to interrupt all the time; is likely to throw a tantrum if her demands are not satisfied instantly; will demand attention *now*; will create havoc if asked to

wait one minute; will always want to be the centre of attention, and will play
the fool to get it.

The negative-attention trap

There is nothing unusual about children wanting all the attention they can
get. The attention they like best is praise and active interest. But negative
attention – the sort they get when they are naughty – is better than no
attention at all.

Attention that kids want

Praise and interest are best   ☺

Negative attention is second-best   ☺

No attention – can't stand it!   ☹

All young children can be naughty, just to keep a parent's eyes focused on
them. But, in time, most learn how to get positive attention by being good.
Positive attention is better than the negative kind, so being good gets to be
more common than being bad. What is unusual about children with ADD is
that they appear to stay hooked on naughty, negative attention-seeking
behaviour throughout their childhood. They don't grow out of it the way
other children do. This is the Negative-Attention Trap!

ADD children get caught in the Negative-Attention Trap because it is so
hard for them to please you by being good. If it were easy for them to play
quietly for ten minutes or do as they are told, they would do this to please
you, but it isn't. When they do try to be good they usually get things wrong.
And they so often get it wrong that they tend to receive far too little positive
attention to feel really secure – even in the most loving household.

But like all children they learn quickly that disruptive behaviour does
grab your attention. It's not the best kind of attention, but it *is* attention, and
it's *easy* for them to get it. So they lap it up. Bad behaviour gets them noticed,
and being noticed makes them feel important. Bad behaviour also tends to
mean that less is expected of them, which means fewer demands are made of
them to do the things they find most difficult. For example:

It is time for Harry (aged six) to put his toys away ready for his bath and then bed. His mum, Karen, asks nicely, 'Put your toys in the box, please.'

Ten minutes later he is playing on – he is wrapped up in the game; he doesn't want a bath.

Mum raises her voice: 'I told you to put those away!'

Harry now throws a tantrum, hurling Lego around the room. Mum is now *shouting* at Harry. At the same time she is going around the room *tidying up the mess* he has created.

In one simple outburst Harry has:

- gained masses of attention

- delayed the bath

and

- has Mum all to himself.

Making the change

Shouting, arguing and smacking do not stop naughtiness because they are still types of attention – they result from the child being naughty in the first place. Paradoxically, punishment may actually 'reward' the bad behaviour. Negative attention-seeking will have become a deeply ingrown pattern which is rarely changed by medication alone, and certainly not by an appeal to the child's reason.

To pull your child out of the Negative-Attention Trap you must adopt a twofold approach:

1. You must reward good behaviour like crazy, making it as easy as possible for her to get positive attention – the best kind. And you are already doing this.

2. You must stop 'rewarding' her with your attention for being naughty.

Your motto from now on must be: Starve the bad (of attention) and feed the good (with attention and praise).

What to ignore and what *not* to ignore

Every time you give attention to silly, irritating behaviour your child spots the way to keep your attention focused on her. Because it works she will do more of it. If it stops working, she will do less of it, especially if she is increasingly able to get your attention by behaving well. From now on you need to be much more selective over the naughty behaviour you respond to.

The recipe is simple: to starve attention-seeking you have to ignore more. It sounds easy, but I know it's not. In practice, ignoring can be a toughie. So you have to be clear about:

- what behaviour you must *definitely ignore*
- what behaviour you must *definitely respond to*.

I can tell you now that you should definitely:

- ° *Ignore* pestering for sweets all the way around the shops
- ° *Ignore* her rude demands to have her own way instantly
- ° *Ignore* silly tantrums when she doesn't get her own way
- ° *Ignore* silly habits designed to get on your nerves and grab lots of attention, like flicking food at the table.

But there are things you can't ignore:

- ° *Don't ignore* a risk that she might hurt herself.
- ° *Don't ignore* something that could hurt others.
- ° *Don't ignore* actions that might destroy something you can't replace.

Protection must be your priority and you must always act to **make the situation safe**. You have no choice.

The following table illustrates these issues. It is a record of 15 minutes of interaction between Helen and her son Harry in their own home. Helen wanted help to cut down the dire problems she was having with Harry's defiance. As a first step I needed to assess whether she was actually rewarding Harry's attention-seeking behaviour with too much attention.

Time	What Harry did	What Helen did in response
8 a.m.	Refuses his breakfast. The milk is too warm.	Helen throws the breakfast in the bin. Offers other options – which Harry refuses one by one. 'What are you going to have, then?' she repeats each time he refuses.
8.03	Wants crisps…repeats over and over, 'I want crisps'.	Helen stops helping 3-year-old Ronnie choose his breakfast so as to deal with Harry. She explains 5 times to Harry, 'No breakfast, no crisps.' She repeats this every time he says, 'I want crisps.'
8.05	Harry tries to get into the cupboard where the crisps are kept. Can't reach, so he kicks the wall. His voice is very loud – he is screaming: 'GET THE CRISPS!'	Helen shouts back, 'Stop shouting…you're not getting them.' Ronnie is now irritable because Mum isn't listening to him.
8.08	Harry is in the lounge, turning the TV on and off repeatedly and looking directly at Helen for a reaction.	Helen screams to Harry: 'Do that once more and you'll see what I'll do!'
8.10	Looking at Helen, he switches the TV on and off, grinning.	Helen chases Harry – he runs away laughing. She chases him into the kitchen.
8.12	Harry grabs Ronnie's hair and pulls hard.	Helen grabs Harry and smacks him hard. She picks up Ronnie, who is crying.
8.14	Harry laughs at Helen to show 'it didn't hurt'. He goes back to the TV and switches it on and off again.	She puts Ronnie down. Walks to the TV and removes the plug and the lead. She turns her back on Harry.
8.15	He throws himself on the floor in a tantrum.	Helen ignores him.

The sequence may be somewhat familiar. But what could Helen do to change this situation?

First, notice the number of silly wind-ups that Harry uses to get attention in the first few minutes. They are designed to get Helen focused on him, not Ronnie. Unfortunately, Helen falls for it every time. She always responds to his provocation. Instead of ignoring it, she rewards his attention-seeking and he simply does more of it.

Second, notice that only at the end of the 15 minutes – when everyone is tense and upset – does she use *the only weapon she has* against Harry's attention-seeking – which is to ignore it.

Third, Helen is absolutely superb both when she removes the TV lead – thereby ending the source of the wind-up – and when she follows it up by turning her back and ignoring the tantrum.

As we discussed this sequence, Helen realised that she needed to *starve all the nonsense* of its attention-pulling power. I encouraged her to look for any opportunity she could find to *boost the positives* in Harry's behaviour outside of times when the two of them are arguing or fighting. This meant spotting *every time* Harry was cooperative or sensible.

One other thing Helen could not ignore was Harry's pulling Ronnie's hair! She *had to* intervene and take action. However, there were many opportunities – both before and after this incident – to ignore Harry's behaviour, and she was wholly right when she finally ignored the tantrum that followed.

TIP FOR SUCCESS

- Consistency wins the day (see Golden Rule No. 4– Be Consistent, page 41). Many parents pick the right issue to ignore and the right time to ignore it, and then throw it all away by not following through when their child tests them out.

The uphill battle

A child in the Negative-Attention Trap is an expert at doing things that really get to you; things you find so hard to ignore. Because of a long history of troublesome behaviours many parents find that they are on the lookout for signs of trouble and react very quickly and 'overfocus' on these behaviours. Unfortunately, this reinforces the same old message to the child: 'To get

Mummy's and Daddy's attention – be naughty!' Remember, always be on the lookout for good behaviour.

CLOSE down

Starving naughtiness of its attention-grabbing potential means you must *ignore it with conviction*. To help you remember, I use the phrase, 'CLOSE down', which is exactly what you must do to carry your message home:

C is for **Cut off conversation**. Don't say another word until you are ready.

L is for **Look away**. No eye contact.

O is for **Offer no reaction**. Whenever possible, do not react to attempts to draw you into arguments or discussions that show your child that you can be sucked back into the game.

S is for **Switch off smiles**. This can be the hardest thing for a loving parent. But do not give in to his or her attempts to make you laugh or smile.

E is for **End when you're ready**. Don't be dictated to by your child. Stop ignoring only when you feel satisfied that you are getting your message across.

This all sounds very harsh, I know, but in the context of a caring relationship 'closing down' is not only far more effective, it is less damaging to a child than either smacking (where you have, in effect, lost control) or nagging (where you undermine his or her self-confidence).

Pitfalls and new approaches

Use the space below to jot down any of the pitfalls you are aware of in the ways you are currently dealing with attention-seeking.

✎ . . . .

. . . .

. . . .

. . . .

. . . .

. . . .

. . . .

. . . .

. . . .

Then write down at least one of the suggestions above that is new to you and that may be useful for **improving your approach** during the week ahead:

✎ . . . .

. . . .

. . . .

. . . .

. . . .

. . . .

. . . .

. . . .

Remember: the effort that you put into your communication skills will be repaid in your own growing confidence and in the fact that you are clarifying things for your child.

Frequently asked questions

Q: *'Ignoring a determined child can be very wearing. How do I keep it up time and time again?'*

A: Try keeping your mind focused on your long-term goals for permanent change and not on the short-term relief or easy option that giving in or backing down can bring. Make regular use of your powerful motivators, developed in Step 1.

Q: *'How can I tell if I'm improving in my communication?'*

A: One way is to observe the difference in your child. If you're having no impact, you're missing something. Another is to get feedback from someone else. As odd as it may sound, I recommend to all my clients that they find someone they trust to observe their efforts in communicating. This person might be your partner or one of your parents, but more likely it will be a trusted friend who understands what you are trying to achieve and will give you a balanced evaluation of your efforts.

RECAP

To change attention-seeking:

Reward	Ignore
Anything your child does the first or second time of asking.	Silly attempts to get an audience, e.g.: • demanding crisps instead of breakfast • shouting, kicking furniture.
Any attempt to please you or do things your way.	Tantrums when she can't get her own way.
Anything she does that you would like to see more of, e.g.: • looking at a book for 5 minutes • not moaning when asked to...	Doing something she is not to, which she knows annoys you, e.g.: • flicking the TV on and off • repeating the same stupid comment over and over.

FINAL TIP FOR SUCCESS

- Plan ahead for known crunch points when negative attention-seeking is likely to be at its worst – times like getting ready in the morning, mealtimes, bath times and bedtimes. These are the moments when you are likely to be most stretched and least able to cope with naughtiness. And your child knows this full well. So be prepared by having ready a range of activities that will hold her attention for short periods. This way you can divert her away from attention-seeking mischief by keeping her mind occupied.

Keep an eye on what is happening, and be ready to switch to some new activity just before the point when she is getting a bit twitchy and restless. Draw up a list of activities to fill stressed times with distraction and stimulation:

Extra things to do

1. 10 minutes' video

2. Cutting up bread for the birds

3. Stuffing the old newspapers into a rubbish bag

4.

The Secret of Commands

Amazing! Step 6 – half way and you're still reading. Allow me to congratulate you.

Everything we have covered so far has been aimed at boosting a positive approach to the management of your child's behaviour. Now is the time to introduce the limits and boundaries that ADD children find so hard to deal with.

In Step 6 we will explore the topic of delivering effective commands. I am confident that you will soon be an expert. You will:

- learn to identify disempowering commands – that is to say, vague, 'flooded', question and plea commands, and the sort that start with 'Let's' and 'We'll'.

- find alternatives that are more potent and more assertive

- discover how to assert yourself effectively with your child.

Clarify the message

'All the world's a stage', and all parents have an audience – a child who is constantly reading the messages you give off, verbal and non-verbal. As a parent you need to play many roles: the toughie, the comforter, the organiser, the referee and the dictator. We have to play them even when we don't feel like it. That is the responsibility of parenthood. The question is – do you play each role to the best of your ability?

What we actually communicate and what we *think* we communicate are not necessarily the same. Actions speak louder than words. When we send messages out to others through our words, gestures, tone of voice and so on, we hope that we pass on what we mean clearly and effectively. There is always a chance that our message may be received as something different from what we intended.

Have you ever found yourself saying something to someone and getting the opposite reaction to the one you expected? Maybe you told a sad tale and it provoked a smile. Perhaps you were talking normally and were told to 'calm down'. Has anyone ever come up to you and said, 'Cheer up' when you felt fine, or 'What are you so happy about?' when you didn't know you were? These simple examples illustrate that we cannot always be 100 per cent sure that our communication skills are up to scratch. Oh, sure, sometimes it's them and not you, but sometimes it *is* you and that's what I will be looking at improving here.

Talking tough and sounding weak will confuse any child – especially a child with ADD. You have to make your actual message match your intended message. That means not only talking firm and decisive but also *appearing* firm and decisive and *being* firm and decisive. Consistency is the byword with ADD children: both consistency of verbal and non-verbal communication and consistency over time.

There are probably good reasons why your messages are sometimes mixed. For example:

- You may fear you will damage your child if you are stern or frosty.

- You may worry that you will make her hate you if you stand firm and don't relent.

- You may be reminded of issues from your own past – e.g. being bullied, unloved or neglected.

- You may remind yourself of your mother or father, and you want to be different.

- You may be uncertain that you are doing the right thing.

These feelings of guilt, distress or uncertainty will almost inevitably show themselves in your body language. They may prevent you from getting the job done effectively.

It's hard to get her to do as she is told

ADD kids resist commands because they think they can't succeed and find it simpler to force you to back down. You are trying to counteract this by pointing out to your child how often she pleases you and how successful she can be. However, in the weeks ahead there is no escaping the fact that you will need to assert yourself. From now on there will be many, many times when you need to set limits firmly and enforce them. So practise in giving no-nonsense commands is a priority at this point.

The three key guidelines to issuing commands

1. If you are going to give a command, think first whether you are prepared to make sure it is carried out. Remember that the difference between a command and a request is that you are not prepared to give in or do it yourself.

2. Commands work best when you have your child's attention. Call her name and wait until she is looking at you before you tell her what you want.

3. Allow her time to comply. Children always test out their parents to see if they really have to do a task. Don't be impatient. Always give your child time to begin the task before you jump in with another command.

A new approach based on these guidelines is not difficult to learn. *Keep your commands short and use language your child can understand* (this applies at almost any age).

First, you must beware of using ineffective commands – a trap that so many parents fall into. These are the types of command to avoid:

- vague
- 'flooded'
- question
- the sort that start with 'Let's' and 'We'll'
- plea.

Avoid vague commands

Look at the following example:

'Put your toys away.'

This command is too vague. It doesn't specify what needs to be done. Unless you spell out exactly what you want, how can the child be sure she's obeying you?

A clearer message might go like this:

'Put your toys away. I want the dolls in the box and the bricks in the jar, and I want them both under your bed. I will be back in five minutes.'

This is far more effective.

Avoid 'flooded' commands

These are the sort that give too much information at once, such as:

'I want you to put your toys away now. Don't mess around as usual, leaving things around for me to pick up … And don't come down till you've done it! I've told you three times and this is your last warning.'

Giving one command *vaguely* is bad enough, but this parent goes on giving more and more instructions. I call these 'flooded' commands because the information just keeps on coming. A lot of it is irrelevant. Stringing different ideas together in this way will confuse the younger child. The verbiage doesn't clarify the instruction – only dilutes it.

Avoid flooding your commands with comments such as:

'If I have told you once I have told you a thousand times.'

'When will you learn? Eh – answer me! When will you?'

Instead:

'Toys away now! I will be back in five minutes'

is usually sufficient.

TIP FOR SUCCESS

- Always pause a little before commanding, so as to be clearer about what you are going to say. Then be succinct.

Avoid question commands

Here are some examples of question commands:

Parent: 'Are you going to hang your uniform up or not? Let's get it over with now, shall we?'

Child: 'No!'

Parent: 'Are you listening to me? Are you going to do as you're told?'

Child: [silence]

Parent: 'Why are you acting like this? Do you want to make me cross?'

Child: 'Don't know.'

Have *you* lost sight of what the task is? This child clearly has. The classic mistakes here are mixing questions and commands together. I know that parents use questions like this to develop their children's reasoning skills and get them to reflect. But don't do it when you are trying to give commands.

A command is not a question. You want it done and you want it done now. So turning it into a question is redundant and confusing. This parent has got the child thinking about Mum's feelings rather than focusing on hanging up his uniform!

I suggest 'Hang up your uniform' will be more effective.

Avoid 'Let's' and 'We'll'

'Let's tidy the crayons away. C'mon, we want to be a good boy for Mummy, don't we?'

'Let's brush our teeth now, shall we?'

'We'll get dressed on time this morning, won't we?'

Phrases like 'Let's ...' and 'We'll ...' are fine as long as you intend to join in and they aren't just commands in disguise. Many parents say, 'Let's' and 'We'll' when what they really mean is 'Do it.' They are then puzzled and annoyed when their child expects them to take a hand or do it for them.

TIP FOR SUCCESS

- If you actually think your child may need help, make it clear that help is available if she asks for it. For example:

  'Do your teeth, sweetheart – if you have problems, just ask me.'

Avoid plea commands

'I would be very grateful if you would stop kicking!... *Please.*'

Never mix up a command with a plea. Be straight and to the point.

Pitfalls and new approaches

Use the space below to jot down any pitfalls – ineffectual ways of giving commands that you recognise in yourself.

✍ . . . .

. . . .

. . . .

. . . .

. . . .

. . . .

. . . .

. . . .

. . . .

. . . .

. . . .

As a reminder for the week ahead, write down an alternative approach.

✍ . . . .

. . . .

. . . .

. . . .

. . . .

. . . .

- Get your voice right – sound serious and firm. But avoid sounding angry or aggressive, or getting agitated and red in the face. This will make your task harder. Why? Well, from the child's point of view, getting uptight and agitated suggests that you are already cross with her. And if you are already cross, why should she try to please you by doing as she is told?

Frequently asked questions

Q: *'This all sounds a bit dominating and bossy to me.'*

A: You're right. If this were your main way of communicating with your child, then it would be oppressive for him. I am only suggesting that you use the right tools for the job at the right time. There are times when you have asked nicely and politely, and been patient, but to no avail. A child defying you in this way won't be moved or helped by more of the same. I am suggesting that you have to act firmly and decisively.

Q: *'My child gets upset with the "new" me and that makes me feel guilty.'*

A: Being firm can upset you and your child, particularly if you are experimenting with new ways of issuing commands. But maybe we need to tease out the issues here. If you have set limits in an appropriate way there is nothing to feel guilty about. If you are still feeling guilty, then don't show it to him. It's a mixed message.

But what if you are *still* feeling guilty about your child's reaction to the limits you set?

Ultimately it is not your limits that are being tested, but your resolve. In other words, your limits are not at fault; what your child wants to do is test your ability to enforce them and then stick to your guns. This is Negative-Attention Trap territory! If you are finding this test of your resolve hard to bear, then there are a couple of things you can do:

1. Gather support around you, so as to help you feel better about seeing your limits through to the end.

2. Check out some new motivators (see Step 1) that enable you to prevail when the going gets tough.

Q: *'What about negotiation, and what about listening to children?'*

A: Listening and negotiating are often taken to be the same thing. They aren't. I am not suggesting that you should never negotiate with your child. But if a task must be done and done now, negotiation doesn't come into the equation. Asking politely, waiting and trying again are all forms of negotiation. Only do these things if you are really prepared to negotiate – which means you are prepared to concede on the right terms. If it's not negotiable, don't negotiate.

Listening, however, is crucial at all times. I urge you, even when you are in the midst of giving commands, to listen to your child:

- Give him your full attention.
- Don't interrupt or speak over him.
- Demonstrate that you have heard and understood.

But unless something you have heard has swayed you, simply say, 'I understand what you mean [what you are saying] but I want you to clear this mess up now [or whatever]. We can talk about that later.'

FINAL TIP FOR SUCCESS

- After you have been successful in following through a command, explanations about the stand you have taken can go a long way towards defusing any bad atmosphere. In my experience children of all ages value and respect the fact that you take the trouble to talk it over with them, even if they don't show it. 'Talking it over' should not be about getting them to like or agree with your decision, so avoid renewing any argument about it. The aim is to model how respect is shown to individuals, whatever the differences between them.

Task Wars

Welcome back. You're working hard. You are:

- organising Special Times

- running the Home Points System

- praising like crazy

- ignoring attention-seeking

- delivering effective commands.

The good news is that there are no exercises in this section; the only task is reading.

Today we investigate the causes of **task wars.** You will:

1. read about why ADD children struggle emotionally and practically with routine tasks

2. discover a new way of understanding the mechanism by which you and your child get into conflict over tasks.

This information will prepare you for Step 8, where you will be urging your child to organise himself and tackle tasks daily.

The problem with 'things-to-do'

There are things to do every day: getting up on time; putting things away; leaving a room tidy behind you; going to bed at a reasonable time. It's a long list. Most of them are just routines: actions we repeat over and over. For adults they become habits that we don't even think about; but all children need help to get to that stage, and ADD children need extra help.

Many ADD children consistently fail when it comes to things-to-do and get aggressive and argumentative about doing them. This can make their time with their parents full of stress and conflict. Being organised is helpful. It makes life easier.

Task wars: Why are things-to-do hard for ADD children?

Typically, things-to-do signal big areas of conflict between ADD children and their parents. In many respects ADD children are just like other children when it comes to chores. They find them boring and dislike being asked to do them. All children have to learn that chores are part of life, and they all rebel at times. So some rebellion is normal for ADD children and not part of their condition.

However, for ADD kids daily tasks are particularly difficult because they are made up of things that they are not good at such as concentrating, avoiding distraction until the task is finished, remembering what comes next, and controlling the urge to do something more interesting.

Usually, when we teach children daily tasks it goes like this: 'I demonstrate it, then you do it, then you repeat it.' But this does not work so well for ADD kids. They pick up how to do the task easily enough – ADD children are often bright and learn new skills quickly – but the ADD makes repeating what they have learned, in the same order and without getting distracted, hard – even something taught to them just minutes before! So what should be a doddle becomes arduous.

Things-to-do: What it means for ADD children

Failing =	Succeeding =
lower self-esteem	self-confidence
arguments at home	feeling on a par with others
feeling they can't please adults	being able to build on successes
feeling they are to blame.	feeling in control.

Martine and Dominic

ADD children not only fail at things-to-do, they also get aggressive and tantrummy when they do.

Martine has this problem with her seven-year-old son Dominic. 'I have always felt that I had to nag Dominic to get things done. I would expect him to get on and do things, but as soon as I turned my back he would be doing something else. Then when I reminded him, World War Three would break out. He was just four or five then, but he would refuse point-blank to do as he was told. Even if I asked nicely, "Please tidy your room", he would "go into one". The whole street must have heard the rows we had.'

Many parents report similar experiences. Just mentioning that a job needs doing can lead to an outburst.

Martine and Dominic are a classic example of how the trouble starts. Martine didn't know for quite a while that Dominic had ADD. She had the same expectations of him as of her older son Nathan, who doesn't have ADD. She expected jobs to be done without fuss. She naturally compared the two boys. She didn't have to nag Nathan – he just got things done. She concluded that Dominic was naughty and defiant. Dominic once told me, 'I don't know why but I could never get things right for my mum. I used to say I didn't know why I forgot things. She didn't believe me. So I got to hate her for picking on me. It felt unfair.'

From the start Dominic's ADD always held him back, particularly when it came to organising himself and doing jobs. He wanted to please his mum, but the way he behaved meant he never managed it. He felt more nagged and criticised than his brother. Dominic is a sensitive and loving boy. But he felt he wasn't as good as his brother and he resented the nags and got angry. By the time he was four, he was questioning how much his mum loved him. He appeared to have given up trying to please her.

Every time Martine nags it acts as a *trigger* for these feelings. Dominic shouts and lashes out to avoid the tasks he finds hard and detests. The words 'Tidy ... room' can be enough to set off his temper. The wilder he gets, the less Martine feels like asking. He feels more isolated than ever.

Understanding Dominic's response

Dominic is insecure and lacks self-esteem. His best form of defence is attack. He learned a long time ago that if he shouted really loudly his mother would back off. At first a small tantrum would put her off trying to make him do as he was told. Now she is getting tougher with him, and he produces more severe and more persistent outbursts to keep from doing as he is told. It works, so he keeps it up.

Understanding Martine's response

Martine never sees Dominic succeeding, or helping her. She expects failure and feels frustrated. She feels dominated by her son's tantrums. She knows Dominic is getting away with too much, but his tantrums are so extreme that they seem like 'fits' to her and they overwhelm her. She is angry inside. During their arguments she says things she doesn't mean and sometimes she lashes out. She blames herself, and is at her wits' end over what to do.

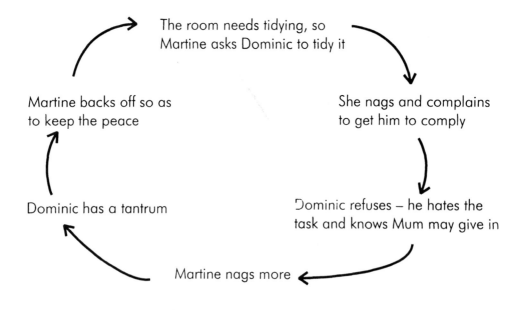

The room needs tidying, so Martine asks Dominic to tidy it

She nags and complains to get him to comply

Martine backs off so as to keep the peace

Dominic refuses – he hates the task and knows Mum may give in

Dominic has a tantrum

Martine nags more

Dominic's and Martine's pattern

Task peace

If your aim is:

- to get your child to succeed where in the past he failed

- to stop him feeling criticised and marginalised

- to show him you understand and want to help

– here's what must happen:

1. You must get your child organised. To do this you will need to break down a task into a schedule – a simple sequence of steps that he can follow. How you do this is explained in Step 8.

2. Both of you must *interrupt* the behaviour pattern that leads to rows. This means drastically reducing the number of confrontations between you when things are said and done that you don't mean – the rest of this section outlines how to do this.

3. Praise must again become your secret weapon (see Step 4).

Make a fresh start

Here are some new motivators that you could try, to help you make changes as far as things-to-do are concerned:

- 'I take each day at a time.'

- 'Each day is a fresh start, and my efforts will work.'

- 'I'm keeping up the positives, blocking out the negatives.'

- 'He's going to enjoy these schedules, and I'm going to benefit. I am determined.'

- 'There's no going back.'

- 'I shall starve the nonsense, and feed what I want more of.'

Avoid the road to rows

These are the key things you must do to help things along:

- Be positive, even if inside you have loads of doubts about your ultimate success.

- Describe the new approach in positive terms.

- Try to be inventive. Make the new approach sound fun and interesting, like a game.

- Try to keep positive even if your positiveness is thrown back in your face. Get into the habit of instilling hope in your child: 'OK, we didn't get that far today. You'll crack it tomorrow.'

- Be calm – especially in the first two weeks when he may try to sabotage your efforts by drawing you into the old arguments.

- Always remember your long-term goal: to reduce the amount of anger, complaining and criticism that your child is exposed to.

- Be firm with yourself. Avoid being critical and saying something you know you shouldn't. It will just confirm for your child that *you can't change…so neither can he.*

- Do not nag, criticise or confront. If you do, he will react as before. Try your best to stop yourself when you feel you are going to do it. In place of a nag or a moan try:

  - teasing or joking: 'The list is watching you – get on with it.'

  - appealing to his sense of achievement: 'C'mon – I know you can do this. Look at the way you fixed your friend's bike yesterday.'

  - appealing to his competitive side: 'You're not going to let ADD be the boss of this schedule are you?'

  - reminding him of the incentives: 'C'mon, I want you to get those points – it's worth X or Y to you.'

- Praise any behaviour that you would like to see more of.

Remember always, *praise is the most important tool you have to motivate your child.* If he has done something you want to see more of, then you must show you have noticed and get others to notice too. Do not slip into the habit of saying nothing if it is going well and only pointing out when things go wrong – it's all too easy to do this.

Frequently asked questions

Q: *'Should I give points to ensure a positive start?'*

A: Great idea. Feelings of anger and frustration have surrounded the issue of doing tasks in the past. There are many ways in which the Home Points System can be used to get things off to a positive start.

Q: *'Isn't that bribery?'*

A: No. Don't confuse bribes with rewards.

A reward is promised *before* a child is asked to do something. It is meant to encourage. But it also shows you know what you are about and that you are planning in advance. Rewards place the responsibility on the child: 'I want you to get involved in the schedule – I know you can do it. As long as you show me a big effort [spell out the details] today, I'll give you the points for the computer game.'

A bribe is offered *after* the child has refused to do something, as a way of buttering him up. Avoid that at all costs. It shows you have lost the initiative and are now dependent on his next move.

Bribes put you one down: 'You said you would give the schedule a chance. I thought we talked about this and you promised ... Look, I'll give you a hundred points if you make a big effort.' The child is still free to reject your offer and, in effect, to get something out of non-compliance.

TIPS FOR SUCCESS

- All these actions depend on your swallowing a lot of feelings of irritation and frustration, keeping them inside, and not 'losing it' – otherwise, you reinforce the old patterns. Your role is to encourage your child to stick to the schedule that you have agreed together.

- Persevere. It will take time, but trust me – it *will* work.

Read on to find out exactly what you need to do.

Mastering Things-to-Do

Now you are ready to help your child manage the routine tasks he has to do.

RECAP

- Most things-to-do aren't optional – they have to be done. This may lead to conflict – possibly quite a lot. However, resolving the difficulties concerning your child's attitude to things-to-do will boost his self-esteem and lower the tension between you.

In Step 8 you will:

- be shown how to draw up a task schedule – there are six key actions involved.
- learn to defuse conflicts over jobs you want your child to do
- build his self-confidence by helping him to manage tasks more effectively.

These strategies combined, will:

- stress his strengths rather than his weaknesses
- limit the conflicts between you.

Targeting things-to-do

The solution to all the problems thrown up by things-to-do is to get your child organised. To do this you will need to:

- break down each task into a simple sequence of steps that he can follow
- put it into writing and get it on display; if your child can't read fully, try little diagrams to show what needs to be done

- give him support and back-up for those times when his mind starts to wander

- add the tasks to your HPS so that they can be noticed and your child rewarded when he has achieved them.

Start today: Draw up your schedule

Taking the sting out of things-to-do for you and your ADD child starts with designing a schedule.

Key action 1 – list the things-to-do

Make a list of the tasks that are causing a problem every day.

Problem things-to-do

1. Getting up on time

2. Putting school uniform away

3. Being ready for bed at 9 p.m.

4. Tidying room

5. Brushing teeth

6. ✎

Key action 2 – pick an easy one

To start with, set yourself up for a quick win by choosing a task that you are committed to changing right away but that is also one of the easiest. It will help you and your child if you score a goal easily first time. For some parents, this might be tidying his bedroom; for others, getting up on time. Remember, only one problem at a time – you are not going to solve everything at once.

Key action 3 – draw up the schedule

Draw up a schedule that describes how the task in question would ideally get done. For example, if tidying his room is a problem, it might look like the one Martine drew up for Dominic.

Dominic's schedule

Every Saturday I clean my room. I watch TV until 'Live and Kicking' finishes at 10 a.m. Then, upstairs in my room:
I find any dirty washing – clothes, bed sheets and pyjamas – and put it outside my door.
   I put away all of my things from the floor into the crate under my bed – ready for Mum to hoover.
   Next, I empty my rubbish bin.
   I put any books away on the shelf – so Mum can clean.
   I pull the bed together.
   I put dirty cups in the kitchen.
   Final look – does it look better? Yes – great!

Worth 50 points

It should contain all the things that need to happen and the order you want them done in. Dominic hasn't learned to tell the time yet, so Martine has drawn a clock face to help him be clear about what to do when. (Don't forget to use pictures if your child doesn't read yet.)

   Now this child knows exactly what he should be doing whenever his mother calls to him, 'Dominic, how are you getting on?'

This is looking good. But the schedule might still need changes. Ask yourself: Have I written the schedule clearly? Does the order reflect the best way to get the job done? For example, are there any gaps – periods of time that are not filled? Martine has made sure that every minute is accounted for so that Dominic knows exactly what he should be doing to the precise minute. Is your schedule as precise?

Have you timetabled any free spaces? It's the natural tendency for an ADD child to get distracted and dawdle. So plan for this in your schedule. Give him slots of free time (five minutes long) and encourage him to use it. This will make going through the schedule less arduous for him.

Key action 4 – discuss it with your child

So far, so good. The next step is to discuss the schedule with your child. I believe in consulting (which is different from *telling*) the child about any changes that are being made in his life. Only if his parents involve him will he have a chance to show them how bright and creative he can be. The tricks at this point are these:

1. Emphasise that you are doing this to *help* him with his ADD. This means that you are not blaming him for all the rows and problems you have been having. It shows that you want the two of you to sort out the ADD together.

2. Encourage him to change the schedule you have made. This way you will have captured his interest; he is part of the plan; and you can include him in discussions if things don't work out.

Key action 5 – make a final draft

With all these suggestions in mind, draw up a final draft. Martine's looked like this:

Every Saturday I clean my room. I watch TV until 'Live and Kicking' finishes at 10 a.m. Then, upstairs in my room: I find any dirty washing – clothes, bed sheets and pyjamas – and put it outside my door.

I put away all of my things from the floor into the crate under my bed – ready for Mum to hoover.

Next, I empty my rubbish bin.

I put any books away on the shelf – so Mum can clean.

I pull the bed together.

I put dirty cups in the kitchen.

Final look – does it look better? Yes – great!

Worth 50 points

Sat 10th	Sat 17th	Sat 24th			
✓					

You have now taken the first step towards organising your son or daughter. You will notice that Dominic's schedule now has a tick box in it. Every day that the task or tasks get completed more or less as set out, Dominic earns a tick. Why? Because you have to demonstrate that you notice when your child is succeeding, and that success must be transferred as points to the HPS so that it can be rewarded. I cannot emphasise enough that you should build in small incentives for getting things right.

Key action 6 – target the rest of the things-to-do
The final stage is gradually to target each of the different problem areas and design new schedules for them. As Dominic achieves progress with one, Martine introduces another – this is her action list:

- Draw up the problem list. Choose one problem.
- Write up the schedule. Revise it.
- Discuss it with your child.

- Display it widely around the house.
- Record success and transfer as points to the HPS. Give incentives.
- Remember, praising success is especially powerful when it comes to getting results.

Now please flick back and re-read 'Task Peace' on page 106.

Frequently asked questions

Q: *'But will my child follow the schedule?'*

A: That's difficult to predict. In most cases one should not expect things to run smoothly at first, but perseverance with this approach works for most people after ten days. Step 9, 'Home Points System: Part 2', explains how you can deal with non-compliance.

Q: *'Doesn't this approach take the spontaneity out of life?'*

A: To some extent, yes, but remember it is your child's spontaneity that at the moment is causing so much frustration. And every piece of research and every bit of evidence on ADD suggest that organisation, timetables and routines worked out with your child are all-important. It's true they don't make for spontaneity, but they will make for a quiet life. And the sense of being trapped will pass, for you and your child alike. You have to be clear and have routines if you want her to overcome the problems presented by this condition.

Q: *'How do I explain this to my child?'*

A: Emphasise that you both have to follow the programme and that it will benefit both of you. Above all be positive. Your child is unlikely to welcome this change, so it is important that you describe the routine in positive terms, emphasising the ways in which it will be helpful. For instance, 'When we keep to the times set out, I can have my breakfast at the same time as you, and you can get to school on time without us ending up in a bad mood with each other.' This underlines the fact that you will be as affected by the routine as she will be.

Q: '*How cool should I be?*'

A: Be firm with her. Do not be pushed around by a child hell-bent on sabotage. Use Time Out if you need to – if she tears up the schedule, for example (see Step 10, 'Time Out for Difficult Behaviours: Part 1').

The Home Points System
Part 2

Still turning the pages! That's excellent. Consider yourself an expert – even if you have adapted the programme to suit your own needs in some way or cut a few corners. Reading this much means that *you know what works and can start educating others.* Go for it.

Step 3 introduced you to the Home Points System. So far, you have been using only one half of its potential. I now want to show you the key actions you need to undertake to get even more out of this powerful tool. Now you introduce a new element to the HPS: an agreement that points earned can be lost if simple and basic expectations are not met.

'Less-of' behaviours

'Less-of' behaviours will generally be the things you have moaned about a couple of hundred times. The version of the Home Points System that you have been using up to now has encouraged you and your child to find ways of earning rewards for maintaining 'good' behaviour and completing tasks effectively. Hopefully, he has earned and you have given some rewards. Ideally, he is reaping the benefit of scoring high points. Over the next pages you will radically change the HPS. It will start to reflect the need for your child to think about others and accept that he cannot have everything all his own way. He is ready for this challenge because you have:

- strengthened the bond between you

- rewarded him for just being him

- praised him through the roof

- encouraged every effort he has made

- supported him in his attempts to get organised

- been patient when it counts.

This week you will:

- introduce penalties for behaviour you want to see less of

- clarify your expectations for good behaviour

- keep the HPS in charge.

Targeting the 'less-ofs'

Your HPS chart makes it clear that you encourage and reward the things your child does more of. Now you must spell out the behaviours you want to see less of or not at all. You know that nagging has never produced change, and never will. Nagging is useless with ADD children, but the HPS combined with your beefed-up skills of assertiveness will reap the rewards you are looking for.

Key action 1 – list the 'less-ofs'

Introduce 'less-ofs' in the same way that you set up the HPS at the start, with only 'more-ofs'. So, first on a sheet of paper, make a list of less-ofs. Not too many but enough to get started – say four or five. The same rules apply as with more-ofs. Include only those behaviours that you are certain he or she is capable of stopping if motivated. Things like:

Less-of behaviours

1. Interrupting me on the phone after I have warned you once

2. Using the F word at any time

3. Punching your little brother at any time

4. Climbing over the fence into next-door's garden at any time

5. ✎

Be specific. So don't say things like 'Stop being rude' or 'Don't be immature'. I know this is precisely what you *do* want, but this is our old enemy the vague command. This kind of catch-all wording casts you as a dictator because you haven't spelt out exactly what you want. This will alienate most kids. It smacks of 'I and I alone decide what rude or immature is', and from your child's perspective it means you claim the right to make up the rules as you go along.

To overcome this, list only those behaviours that are observable and specific. For example, 'You will be in the house by four o'clock after school unless you ring first.' And swap vague comments like 'Be polite to my friends' for specific guidelines like 'Say hello when you answer the phone, not "What?".'

Key action 2 – make the less-ofs chart

Here is a new chart that I want you to draw up. Fill in the less-ofs column with the items on your list.

I want to see less of these	Points each costs	Points that you have lost							
		Mon	Tues	Weds	Thurs	Fri	Sat	Sun
Climbing over the fence at any time	10	-							
Thumping your brother at any time	50	100							
Interrupting me while I'm speaking to Dad	2	18							
Points lost		118							

Quite a daunting prospect for an ADD child, isn't it? So proceed with caution.

TIPS FOR SUCCESS

- Let your child know why you are highlighting this change-directed behaviour.

- Keep the penalties low. You don't want him going massively into debt – especially not at the start.

Key action 3 – put it all together

The final step is setting up a way of recording the balance at the end of the day, after points have been earned and lost. See the chart below, which combines the charts on pp.67, 70 and 122.

I want to see more of these	Points each is worth	Points that you have earned						
		Mon	Tues	Weds	Thurs	Fri	Sat	Sun
Out of bed by 7.30a.m.	10 per day							
Load the dishwasher	30 per week							
Brush teeth morning and night	10 per day							
Extra credit								
Total points								

I want to see less of these	Points each costs	Points that you have lost						
		Mon	Tues	Weds	Thurs	Fri	Sat	Sun
Climbing over the fence at any time	10							
Thumping your brother at any time	50							
Interrupting me while I'm speaking to Dad	2							
Points lost								
POINTS LEFT TO SPEND								

Rewards	Points each costs	Points that you have spent						
		Mon	Tues	Weds	Thurs	Fri	Sat	Sun
Staying up for 'Match of the Day'	50							
Extra hour of TV	20							
Picking the video game	180							
No chores to do for today	20							
Total points								

MORE TIPS FOR SUCCESS

- Reward immediately. Remember, behaviour that is reinforced immediately has the best chance of being repeated. Recognise and reinforce a positive behaviour right after it occurs, especially if it is one that has been recently added to the chart. I know I've said this before, but I can't overemphasise its importance.

- Don't nag to get things done. Let the HPS do the work.

- Calculate points daily. Make time to go through the points earned, lost or spent each day. Ensure that your child is there when you do it. It's good for fairness. It's good for his arithmetic skills.

- No loans.

- Don't fall into the trap of engaging in debates and deals to do with the chart. ADD children are bright – they will frequently try to talk you out of a fine and convince you that *they* did right and *you* have got it wrong. Don't argue the toss and don't strike up elaborate deals such as 'OK, not this time, but you must do twice as much homework on Thursday to make up.' How would you

keep track of all these extra demands, anyway? Stick to the rules
you agreed and take points away with no further discussion.

- Avoid a lot of negativity about penalties by holding family
  meetings to revise the chart – especially if there is a big issue to do
  with a particular less-of behaviour. Have some fun. Appoint a
  chairperson who can bring the meeting to order. Take minutes and
  wear hats. Have a tea break with a treat to make the atmosphere
  warm and nurturing. But also make sure the business is done and a
  new agreement is reached that stops silly arguments and niggles.

- Get him to spend, spend, spend. It is a sign of success and an
  incentive for him. As always, give him plenty of opportunities to
  spend his 'cash' and get rewards and privileges.

Frequently asked question

Q: *'Do I use the same ideas with a younger child?'*

A: Yes. The same rules apply. If you are using tokens, taking them away is
the way to spell out that some behaviours have to stop. Explain clearly why
you are doing this and what your child needs to do in the future to prevent
it.

FINAL TIP FOR SUCCESS

- Don't forget, praise and recognition are powerful motivators. Take
  every opportunity to praise your child. Changing is tough!
  Hopefully this is second nature to you by now. But I thought I'd
  mention it, just in case.

Time Out for Difficult Behaviours

Part 1

This chapter contains all you need to know in order to get your own way with your child without resorting to threats, aggression, screaming or losing your temper. It teaches you the effectiveness of the 'Time Out' routine, which will give you:

1. winning strategies for head-to-head confrontations

2. a clear procedure when flash-points occur.

Decide on your strategy

If you have ever felt on the brink of becoming uncontrollably violent with your child (and who hasn't at some time?); if you have ever screamed abuse and said things you felt guilty about afterwards; if you have ever felt you have tried everything and have reached the end of your tether – then this chapter is for you. Having a strategy to handle such situations is important, because we are all prone to losing our temper when under a lot of stress. Parents lashing out physically or verbally is especially confusing for ADD kids because they are constantly being told to control themselves and be less impulsive.

Throughout this programme there will be occasions when your child will throw down an unmistakable challenge: 'I won't do it and you can't make me.' This kind of defiance isn't unique to ADD children, but it is more common with them. At times like these your child requires a swift and appropriate reminder that you are in charge.

By the way, I am not saying you should never smack a child under any circumstances. I am a realist, not an evangelist, and there are occasions when a smack can be appropriate. For instance, stopping a wilful toddler who doesn't understand the danger of traffic with a swift smack on the hand followed by a simple explanation is effective. But the fact that smacking works in these circumstances does not mean it is suitable for the majority of situations. If it looks like becoming your main method of trying to control your child's behaviour, I suggest that something is going very wrong.

The Time Out approach

When a quick punishment is called for, I recommend a technique called 'Time Out'. Pretty soon, threatening Time Out will usually be enough to stop bad behaviour.

Time Out can be used with *any child* between the ages of three and a half and eight. Older children require different approaches that befit their maturity and the complexity of their needs. Older children respond to reasoning; they require options that respect their right to choose a course of action and their ability to recognise the consequences. Withdrawal of privileges and grounding them in a consistent and assertive way appear to be the most effective methods.

For the appropriate age group Time Out should eventually deliver a permanent change in your child's willingness to comply, which means that frequent smacking can become a thing of the past. Families who try Time Out usually adopt it as their main strategy for tantrums and defiance.

Time Out is particularly useful with ADD children because it works by insisting they do the one thing they resist most – sitting still. However, it is not an easy option at the beginning – it can actually be *harder* in the short term.

Time Out works by:

- repetition
- consistency of purpose
- persistence of approach
- determination to succeed.

The Time Out recipe

Ingredients

1 chair (child size)

1 quiet spot in the house (free of TV and toys to play with)

1 child, refusing to do as she had been told

Vast amounts of patience, resolution, determination and self-control

Method

1. Put the chair in the quiet spot. This is now christened 'the Time-Out Chair'. Introduce your child to it. Tell her what it is for. Leave until ready for use.

2. Tell your child, who is now throwing a tantrum and not doing as she is told, 'If you don't stop that ... [e.g. tantrum, pinching] by the time I count to three, I'll put you on the Time-Out Chair'.

3. Start counting out loud, 'That's one...'. Pause a few seconds to see if she stops. If she doesn't, continue: 'That's two.' Your face should be resolute and determined, but not angry. Your voice should be calm – no shouting. If your child has not stopped by 'three!' lead her to the Chair and say these exact words: 'I told you to stop that... [tantrum, pinching, etc.]. Sit on the Chair until I tell you to get off!' Place her on the Chair and walk away.

4. Wait for as long as you judge is right (say about a minute for every year of her age), and when she is quiet tell her she can get off the Time-Out Chair. Then carry on as before.

Sitting on a chair for several minutes is not harmful (despite the dramatic performance you get). It should be well within the capabilities of an ADD child.

5. If your child repeats the same naughty behaviour, pick her up – even if she protests vigorously, and put her back on the Chair. Tell her again: 'I already told you to stop that [tantrum, pinching, etc.]. Sit on the Chair until I tell you to get off!'

   Walk away and ignore.

6. Repeat as many times as necessary.

So let's begin.

Here are the key actions for Time Out. They are so straightforward that for fun I have presented them in a way that any cook would be proud of. But just because it *looks* simple don't be fooled into thinking it *is*. It is definitely *not* easy, and there is plenty I need to tell you to make it a success.

Key action 1 – read the Time Out recipe

As you read I suggest you think about:

- how controlled you will have to be
- how long this process may take
- how repetitive it will be
- the support you may need to follow through.

NOTE

A warning before you set out: do not start the Time Out technique unless you are definitely going to see it right through to the end!

Pause for a moment before you carry on reading. Think carefully about the very first instruction – 'Do not start the technique unless you are going to see it through to the end.' Repetition of Time Out is the key to getting your child to learn. But doing it over and over is very hard work. You really have to persevere. You have to show you mean business. You have to show clearly you will not compromise and will not take no for an answer.

Because Time Out is so demanding of you at the beginning, I suggest that at first you only use it to target the naughty behaviours that are your top priority to shift. By limiting the range of behaviours you apply it to, you will be giving yourself the best chance of being as consistent and resolute as you need to be.

Key action 2 – list difficult behaviours

Go to the list that you produced on page 121. Take from that list any behaviours that have not been shifted by the HPS alone and are still causing conflict. Draw up a new list:

Target these behaviours:

1. Swearing at me

2. Thumping your brother

3. ✎

This is now your action plan. When your child challenges with one of the behaviours on the list, you go into action with Time Out.

How the technique works

I will now take you through the Time Out recipe stage by stage so as to put some more detail on to the bare bones.

---

1. Put the chair in the quiet spot. This is now christened 'the Time-Out Chair'. Introduce your child to it. Tell her what it is for. Leave until ready for use.

A quiet spot is essential. You need to have your child out of the flow of family activity. If she can see the TV or interact with others the impact of Time Out is lost. Do not compromise on this aspect of the technique. Sitting quietly where there is nothing to do or look at is boring. Making her do this *is* the punishment.

The one negotiation you might permit is over what she sits on. The Chair itself is not the punishment. If sitting in the Chair becomes an issue in itself, then consider other places that are equally boring. Getting her to sit on the floor in the hall or on the bottom step of the staircase, or stationing her in a spot at the other end of the room where you happen to be, may all work just as well – providing you are consistent and follow the Time Out technique through in all other respects.

Chair or bedroom?

Sending a child to her room is *not* Time Out. Sending her to her room gives the message: 'Give me a break – get out of my sight.' But it also means a 'break' for her. In her room she can entertain herself. Furthermore, an ADD child is likely to forget the reason for the punishment – or even that it was supposed to be a punishment at all. So no change in behaviour is likely to result.

In contrast, when you use the Chair the message you give is: 'I am watching you and if you keep doing *that*, I will make you do *this*.' Sitting on the Time-Out Chair is the reminder that you want her to learn how to behave and you are willing to keep this up until she responds.

---

2. Tell your child, who is now throwing a tantrum and not doing as she is told, that she has until you count to three to stop being naughty. Say, 'If you don't stop that... [e.g. tantrum, pinching] by the time I count to three, I'll put you on the Time-Out Chair'.

3. Start counting out loud, 'That's one'. Pause a few seconds to see if she stops. If she doesn't, continue: 'That's two.' Your face should be resolute and determined, but not angry. Your voice calm – not shouting. If your child has not stopped by 'three!' lead her to the Chair and say these exact words: 'I told you to stop that... [tantrum, pinching, etc.] Sit on the Chair until I tell you to get off!' Place her on the Chair and walk away.

You may find in the beginning that you need to pick your child up and physically put her on the Chair. She may kick and scream. Be careful neither of you gets hurt. Avoid smacking and threats to get her into the Chair. What is required is that you get her to stay on the Chair long enough for you to give the command. It is actually important that her bottom touches the Chair because that is the prerequisite for everything that follows.

---

4. Wait for as long as you judge is right (say about a minute for every year of her age) and when she is quiet tell her she can get off the Time-Out Chair. Then carry on as before.

Children will often shout, jabber, scream or **whinge** while in Time Out. This is their way of showing that you needn't think things are going to go all your way. If your child is being defiant in this way, insisting that she is quiet *before she come off* is your way of staying in the driving seat.

I recommend that a child is quiet for at least 30 seconds before she gets off.

TIP FOR SUCCESS

- Repeat, repeat, repeat. As I have said, it is the repetition of Time Out that is the key to getting your child to learn. Yes, it is very demanding on you.

Key action 3 – read on?

Now you can make your list of behaviours to be tackled and start using Time Out. But you might want to read Step 11 first – it explores some of the difficulties that parents often experience in the first week of Time Out, and offers some strategies for dealing with them. Reading it now may help you to feel more prepared. However, all parents are different. You will already have an idea of how you and your child are going to find this new approach. You may wish to get stuck in straight away and learn through your own experience before going on to explore more strategies. Please feel free to do this.

Now...

- Make your list of behaviours to be dealt with by Time Out.
- Apply the techniques as closely as possible to the method described.
- When you are ready, read Step 11 for trouble-shooting advice.

Time Out for Difficult Behaviours

Part 2

In my experience Time Out rarely goes smoothly, but being prepared helps. In this chapter I am going to:

- illustrate in more detail the problems you may encounter at the start of Time Out

- prepare you, and advise you on what to do.

Jamie

Delia and Rick have a seven-year-old son, Jamie. Jamie is often defiant and spiteful. Delia was desperate for advice on how to manage his behaviour. I described Time Out, and she agreed to try it at home. A week later she said, 'I couldn't get Time Out to work. Jamie wouldn't sit on the Chair. He ignored my commands to get him there. I stopped because we were heading for a fight, which I was trying to avoid.'

I got Delia to describe in detail what had happened. This is what she told me:

'Lily's [Jamie's eight-year-old sister] friends had come over to play. They let Jamie join in their game of rounders, but when he was 'out' he started to play up. He wouldn't give the bat back and started to hit Lily. Everyone was getting upset. I took Jamie inside – I told him he had until the count of three to give it back or he would be on the Chair. He refused. I took the bat and told him he was on the Time Out Chair. He completely ignored me. He went straight into the garden and caused more trouble. I picked him up and put him back on the Chair, but he would not stay. He ran upstairs. He treated the whole thing like it was a game.'

Delia explained that she gave up chasing him when she felt her temper rising and the desire to smack growing inside her. On other days, too, Jamie responded in a similar way. Delia wanted more advice on what to do.

Lots of parents find their child refuses point-blank to sit on the Chair, won't stay on it, and treats the whole thing as a joke. This kind of difficulty is so common with Time Out that I knew exactly what advice to offer:

'When you reach "Three", you know that Jamie is going to ignore what you say and will not go on the Chair. In the past you have chased him and got wound up. This way he has learned that being defiant gets him lots of attention. Next time he refuses to sit on the Chair, pick him up firmly but safely and put him back on it. Tell him that if he gets off (and you and I know he will), you will ignore him until he sits there properly.

'From then on, Delia, I want you to enforce CLOSE-down as firmly as you can. By this I mean **no eye contact**, **no communication**, **no persuasion**; **offer no drinks**, **no treats** – **nothing** – until he sits on the Chair! This sounds extreme, but if you want to get your message across you must not give in. And you must be prepared to keep it up for as long as it takes.

'The more attention he demands, the less he receives. If you must respond at all simply say "I'm waiting for you to sit on The Chair!"'

I added:

'When Rick comes home explain the situation and get him to back you up by enforcing CLOSE-down too. You can act as normally as possible with other members of the family. But until Jamie sits on the Chair, *for him* nothing changes.'

I advised Delia that few children push the limits beyond an hour or two at the most. Exceptionally, the stalemate can carry on until bedtime. I reassured her that she and Jamie could end the day with stories and cuddles, but she should tell her son that if he played up again the next day he would go on the Chair again.

Delia asked me, 'What do I do if he ups the ante by threatening to hurt himself or me or destroy something in the house? I can't ignore that, can I?'

I agreed with her that there are times when you have to act. You have to prevent your child hurting himself or others. However, I still suggest you try to avoid smacking. All too often this can make things worse. Here are two other ways to regain control of the situation, and a word on smacking – for the times when you think it just can't be avoided.

Action	Pros	Cons
• Hold him firmly but safely.	• This restrains his actions, and the bodily closeness to you calms him down.	• None – except that it **must not hurt** or act as a physical punishment.
• Put him in his room.	• This takes him out of the situation and allows him to calm down on his own.	• None.
• A controlled smack? **Think twice about it.**	• This may startle him out of his temper and help him cry his anger out.	• Quite a few – it may upset him more, your smack may be harder than you think and, if done more than very occasionally, it may give him the wrong message about how to get his own way.

I also suggested to Delia that when things have calmed down she should let Jamie know she understood how upset he had been. She might, perhaps, offer him a drink as they talked things over together.

Remember:

- It is all right to be understanding and caring

- But it is wrong to be apologetic

And Delia should not give up on her request that Jamie sits quietly for a time on the Time Out Chair. When he has calmed down, she should tell him gently but firmly that she now wants him to sit on the Chair so that his Time Out can come to an end. If he refuses, she must start the procedure again until he does.

RECAP

- Once you have started Time Out *you must follow through*. If your child refuses to sit on the Chair, ignore him until he complies. If you have a partner or relative helping you with childcare, he or she must back you up and follow the same line as you.

- If your child looks as though he may harm himself or others, do not attempt to ignore it. *Act!* Take charge of the situation in the way that feels most appropriate and comfortable.

- Remember, after a tantrum has been contained, you must reinforce Time Out. Persist until your child complies.

Delia took my advice, and at our next meeting she told me the difference in Jamie was remarkable. Within thirty minutes of taking this firm line on ignoring, he sat on the Chair and the Time Out followed smoothly through the stages.

Frequently asked questions

Q: '*How do we use Time Out with behaviour problems that happen in public?*'

A: The simple answer is 'Don't'. Using Time Out with an audience of strangers places you in a vulnerable and weak position. It is hard to appear in control while struggling with your feelings of embarrassment. Your child may pick up on this and use the opportunity to become the boss.

Q: '*So how do I cope with problems in the supermarket, at children's parties, restaurants and so on?*'

A: I recommend three simple strategies for behaviour in public.

1. Before you go into a potentially difficult situation such as a visit to a supermarket or restaurant, take time to sit down with your child and spell out clearly what you expect from her. Get her to repeat back her understanding of what she has been told.

2. Tell your child what reward or privilege will follow her compliance with your expectations. This acts as an incentive for good behaviour and positively reinforces the success you may have.

3. Be crystal-clear that there will be a comeback for bad behaviour when you get home, and spell out what it will be. For example, throwing food in a restaurant would mean:

   • points off the Home Points System

   • plus five minutes on the Chair.

   You must, of course, follow this through on your return home. Failing to do so will send out the message 'It's all been forgotten' or 'I don't really mean what I say.' This will leave her confused about what to expect in the future.

Q: '*My child has just broken a treasured possession. How can I use Time Out to show how angry and upset I am and punish her?*'

A: Quite effectively – let's look again at the instructions of the Time Out recipe (page 129). The deed is done – so no point in counting to three! Tell her straight, 'I told you not to touch that. You have broken it and Daddy is very upset. You will sit on the Chair until I tell you to get off.' From then on follow all the advice from instruction 3 onwards.

Q: '*Can I use Time Out for* not *doing something?*'

A: Yes. Very often your child may defy you by not doing a job you asked her to do (e.g. not tidying up). Time Out is useful here as well. Follow instructions 1–6 as usual, and when she gets off the Chair lead her back to the job you have asked her to do and say, 'Now I want you to put your toys in the toy box!'

Q: '*I am concerned that Time Out may upset my child. Should we attempt to patch things up afterwards?*'

A: You're right to have these worries. Although preferable to physical force, Time Out *will* upset your child and the advice I always give is to look for ways to make things up between you after you have used it. Encouraging small gestures that your child can do to please you, such as drawing a card or picture, is often helpful. It gives you a chance to dispel any atmosphere or tension that may have built up and, most important, it gives you an opportunity to praise. Surprisingly, children are happy to do this, probably because it puts them back in charge of their lives again and lets them control the process of making things better between them and their parents.

Q: '*Is Time Out really appropriate for older children?*'

A: There is no doubt that Time Out proves to be very effective with younger children because the learning happens in their formative years. If you are using Time Out for the first time with a child of seven or older you must respect the autonomy and reasoning that she had already gained. Go for punishments that have more meaning for an older child, such as:

- loss of freedom – e.g. grounding her in her room, no friends allowed home
- loss of privileges – e.g. deducting HPS points and pocket money.

Reserve the use of the Chair for those occasions when you need to make a special point about her behaving immature.

For older children the length of Time Out can be extended on each occasion that you have to use it – e.g. six minutes for a six-year-old plus two minutes added for every time she goes back into Time Out. You can also tell an older child that she can end Time Out when she herself decides that she can control her behaviour.

Q: '*How do we manage to stick at Time Out?*'

A: I understand how tempting it can be to give up when progress seems slow. However, in the heat of the moment, when you are being tested to the limit, it is very easy to underestimate the progress you have made. You may be tempted to give up at just the point where it is really beginning to work. At such times it can be all too easy to undermine all the hard work you have put in.

How to avoid smacking

The key to not falling back on smacking and threatening is to make use of the right *motivators*, which I hope you have been finding useful since Step 1. Replacing the old mental messages with new empowering ones can directly influence what you do when you are under pressure. Perhaps you would benefit from another read of Step 1. You might want to review your motivators, or use your regular ones more frequently.

TIPS FOR SUCCESS

Here are the ideas I have used to imprint restraint on to my mind when it comes to smacking:

- As a parent I am a role model for my child.

- Aggression, threats or physical force all model impulsive behaviour – something that we want to see less of.

- Smacking shows my child that I am *out of control*, not in control.

- If smacking worked I wouldn't have to keep doing it.

- Hurting my child damages our relationship.

- *I know a better way!*

Try the anchoring exercise on page 48, with these or with ideas of your own.

Putting It All Together

'You did then what you knew how to do. When you knew better, you did better.'

Maya Angelou

There are no more tasks or strategies. The previous eleven Steps are it.

I know that not all of you will have worked through everything, but for whatever you have managed to put into practice, well done! Allow me to be the first to pat you on the back.

In this chapter we look back at what you have learned, take stock of what you have achieved, and consider what difficulties you may still be facing. We shall also look at setting goals for the future and explore ways you can get more help and support if you need it.

In detail we will review:

- the aims of ADDapt

- how ADDapt works to shape your interaction with your ADD child

- how ADDapt can continue to help you parent him or her

- the other help available to parents.

Give yourself another pat on the back

In my experience, the parents of ADD children are never given the credit they deserve for having coped so well for so long, for not having given up, and for having stuck by their child.

You came to this book looking for answers. You probably felt stuck, at the end of your tether – that you had tried absolutely everything but to no avail.

My aim has been to share some powerful strategies to get you moving again. You should never blame yourself for not knowing things. Remember, none of us parents is ever offered a training in parenting. We can all use some help to improve our effectiveness. Seeking to improve does not mean we have been inadequate. On the contrary, the least inadequate people are those who are always on the lookout for ways to improve.

My work has given me enormous faith in the ability of families to find ways through their difficulties. If you have worked through at least some of this programme and noticed some changes for the better, you will be confirming my faith yet again. If you feel you are still struggling, don't worry – you are not alone. Perseverance is the key. Change will come, I promise.

ADD children: Can't do? Won't do?

My aim throughout has been to stress that learning fresh habits is the key to success. The mindset I have tried to encourage is that there is a huge amount that you as a parent can do to influence how your child behaves.

When it comes to bad behaviour in ADD children, there is a great deal that boils down to bad habits. ADD makes children impulsive, inattentive and hyperactive. It is much harder for them to learn the rules for getting along with other people, and this difficulty is the cause of most of the battles that are waged between you every day. Medication calms ADD children down so that they can learn more easily. But you have to help your child pick up new ways of doing things. To do this *you* have to learn new ways, too.

Parents: Can't do? Won't do?

ADDapt helps you do less of what does not work with your child, and more of what does. Because change is hard for all of us I have offered some powerful new strategies to boost your motivation and determination. These are techniques you can return to at any time. You may also find them useful when rising to other challenges in your life.

If you have not yet tried my suggestions, be prepared to consider them at some time in the future. Most of this book will be relevant and useful to you, when you are ready. You know what you are capable of. You will be the best judge of when the time is right for you.

ADDapt – a companion on your ADD journey

Dealing with ADD is a process that does not stop. We are all prone to slipping back into old patterns. Please think of ADDapt as a long-term companion, not just something you work through once and – hey presto! – you've done it. Its ideas and approaches are ones that you can revisit at any time, when you feel you need them.

I expect that many of you will have dipped in and out of this text, trying techniques and changing them to your own specific requirements. At the risk of repeating myself, this book is designed to be revisited. Many of the steps can be used independently, to boost areas of your relationship with your child as you need to.

I want to glance back for a moment at what you have achieved. ADDapt guides you towards three targets:

- Target 1 – getting closer
- Target 2 – developing new skills
- Target 3 – being in command and under control

Getting closer

Steps 2–4 highlight the 'secret weapons' in your battle to create change:

- spending Special Time together, free of coercion, correction and control
- rewarding with attention, praise and prizes the behaviour you want to see more of
- enhancing your child's strengths through encouragement and building new skills.

These are resources you knew about already but, stuck in the midst of the havoc that life with ADD can bring, you probably lost sight of them. ADDapt gives you permission to make these issues a priority. It has also given you the tools and the guidance to make it happen. The knock-on effect is that your child may have experienced your relationship differently – recognising that you are committed to getting closer to him and to appreciating what he contributes to the relationship.

Developing new skills

Steps 5–8 present the causes of behaviour problems in an ADD child and the strategies for managing them:

- mastering communication with your child

- getting your child organised in a way that empowers him

- learning when to respond and when to ignore.

With ADD children it is especially important that you have the skills to deliver a clear and potent message when you want them to do something your way. The middle stages of the programme concentrate on these issues. If you have had a go at the exercises, then you have already experimented with new ways of getting your message across. You should also be clearer about when it is prudent not to respond.

Revisit these chapters whenever you catch yourself doing what you used to do before. If you have not yet put them to the test, now is your chance.

And if this has whetted your appetite for new ideas and skills, scan the shelves of your local bookshop or library for other titles on communication skills and assertiveness. Often you will come across an idea or technique that you may not have tried before. See the reading list on page 161 for some suggestions.

Being in command and under control

Steps 9–11 present strategies for gaining control of the defiance you are encountering. Parents of ADD children often feel that this is their greatest struggle. Losing your temper in front of your child is demoralising and potentially frightening for both of you. After setting out the strategies for improving the quality of your relationship, ADDapt suggests new ways of remaining in charge. This way you should all be able to cope more easily with the tensions and frustrations that change in this area can provoke.

Using two main techniques – the Home Points System as both an incentive and a deterrent, and Time Out – you develop ways to stop battles for control becoming physical confrontations.

Do you need expert help?

All books have their limitations – even this one! If you feel you need more help, where should you go? Who is there around? What do they offer? How will it help?

A professional meeting you face to face can do something that a book cannot – get to know you personally. Approaching professionals for help requires courage, but the pay-offs can be considerable. The sort of professional you are looking for is a specialist in behavioural problems in children. Child psychiatrists, child psychologists and family therapists and some paediatricians have expertise in this area. They will be familiar with *behavioural modification therapy*, on which ADDapt is based. Some of them may specialise in it or can offer you other therapies that may also be of benefit to you. These may be approaches that work mainly with you and your partner, if you are in a couple; or the whole family together; or just you; or just your child; or you and your child.

My advice is be open to their suggestions. People outside your situation can often spot things that you cannot see, such as habits you are not aware of which may be hampering your attempts at change. They will be able to suggest new ways of looking at things and new solutions to difficulties you have struggled with for years. Try their ideas alongside the ones in this book.

Do you need a support group?

Parents I meet value support groups very highly. There seem to be two main sorts of benefit.

The first is practical advice and information. You get the opportunity to share experiences and ideas with people who have had to face most of the same problems. The support groups that have sprung up around this country are a vital network for distributing important information about ADD and about what is on offer for dealing with it. Our knowledge and understanding of the condition are growing all the time. Linking up with such a group ensures that you hear what the latest thinking is.

Also, if you are coming up against blocks to do with the assessment and treatment of ADD, it is likely that there will be someone in a local group who will have faced those hurdles before you and found a way around them.

The second great benefit is the emotional support and the sense of solidarity given by a group. The people in it will understand exactly what you are going through, and they will be sympathetic when you tell them about the impact ADD has had on your life. They too will have had to deal with the misconceptions of friends and relations who do not know about ADD. They will tell you how much condemnation still comes their way and they will fully understand the value of solidarity in dealing with it.

There is a third benefit. Parent support groups constitute the most powerful lobbies for getting more done about ADD and for getting the condition better understood by schools and other agencies.

Appendix 3 lists the support groups across the UK and their contact numbers.

Final thoughts on success

Each Step has offered 'tips for success'. This final Step seems the right point at which to reflect on *your* success.

First, take credit for having followed this programme in whatever way you have chosen to use it.

Second, take credit also for never giving up on your ADD child. You have worked with this book at a difficult time in your relationship – a time when you felt stuck and possibly very pessimistic about the prospect of change. At this most frustrating of times you have taken steps to help your child and to make a difference. In essence: you have got things moving again.

Whatever your child goes on to achieve in his or her life, one day that fact will, I believe, become of immense importance to both of you.

APPENDIX I

Working in Partnership

For some of us parenting is a partnership. For those of you who do not have a cohabitee or marital partner, there are often people who may influence how you handle your children.

While conflicts and differences are a part of all relationships – particularly when there are kids around – a crucial factor in parenting an ADD child is the ability of the adults involved to work together in a consistent way. The relationship you have with your partner may have the greatest impact on your motivation and ability to make significant changes in your parenting. Working together means that you need to share similar expectations and beliefs about your ADD child, and that you are willing to pull in the same direction to achieve jointly agreed goals.

Because ADD can take a toll on your coping mechanisms, it is common for one or both parents to feel 'defeated' by the problems you have all been experiencing. Frequently, one parent feels more burdened than the other and more pessimistic. There can be many reasons for this pessimism. It is important that you give time and consideration to the issue, because one partner's negativity can undo the positive work of the other.

You can start by identifying when your partner feels defeated. You can normally tell because he or she:

- seems gloomy when thinking about the past, the present and the future

- expresses him/herself in negative ways

- shows no enthusiasm about making change

- shows no hope about things improving

- is more likely to be snappy with the children

- overreacts inappropriately in ways that he or she didn't before

- is extremely irritable when small things go wrong.

If the defeated person I've described sounds like you, let me tell you that you have already taken a first step out of the situation by reading this book (and reading this far). Talking about how you feel will be your second step. This may be to your partner or maybe to someone outside the family such as a trusted friend or colleague. He or she can give you the space to get things off your chest and help you decide whether you need further help. And professionals such as health visitors or GPs – however busy – do recognise the tensions that relationships can be under, and can advise or recommend the right help for you.

Suppose the more defeated person is your partner. There are three things I can suggest you do:

1. Make an opportunity to discuss the issues raised in this book.

2. Take the opportunity to talk over the frustrations that he or she is experiencing. Explain how you feel about where you are with ADDapt. Approach these issues with care. If your partner is feeling vulnerable he or she may react defensively and see you as being critical. Confronting or implying that they are letting you down or not pulling their weight can move you further apart and away from your goal of working together.

3. Discuss the possibility of seeking advice. Talking parenting issues over with someone outside the situation, who is not on either 'side', may be helpful. See Appendix 3 for a list of the agencies that can offer this kind of help.

But remember the old saying about taking horses to water: if your partner does not see the issues as you do and it is hard to talk, do not divert all your energy into cajoling him or her into seeking help. If they do need individual help, then they must get it when it is right for them. What you need to concentrate on now is how you can apply the ideas in this book so that some change can begin in your relationship with your ADD child. Although he or she may pick up that you and your partner are not always working as a team on these ideas, there is much that can still be done. Don't give up because the situation isn't perfect.

Frequently asked questions

Q: 'What if both of us feel defeated at the same time?'

A: Good point. I often think of parenting partnerships like a relay team. As soon as one parent begins to flag, lose patience or energy, the partner needs to take over, giving a break and injecting new energy into the goal that both are aiming it. Sadly, when both partners feel defeated this delicate balancing act breaks down. Feeling this low can often begin a downward spiral, with more and more rows lowering morale further and further. The behaviour of the children may deteriorate at times like these, as they become worried and confused about what is going on. Ultimately the quality of your relationship with your partner suffers and respect for each other can be lost.

It takes honesty to admit that you have fallen into this kind of spiral. You feel vulnerable and sensitive, thinking that you have failed in some way. Outside help is invaluable at times like this. Organisations like Relate have expertise in helping you talk together about your difficulties, in a setting where the usual hostility that may exist between you will be unlikely to surface; this will give you space to share your feelings and to reconnect with your partner. Relationship counsellors, too, are skilled at finding ways of helping people to strengthen their relationships. If you feel that your relationship is experiencing this kind of difficulty, my advice is to wait before starting this programme. Neither of you is likely to succeed in making changes and sticking to them. The timing isn't right. Concentrate instead on steps to build up positive resources in your relationship.

Q: *'What if my partner won't support me in the changes I am making with my child?'*

A: There is no easy answer to this. Ideally, you need to bring your partner along in the efforts that you are making in your relationship with your child. As you begin to re-evaluate how you do things and how you could do them more effectively, you will also be re-evaluating the way your partner approaches the situation. If his or her failure to support you becomes an obstacle to change, then my only advice is that you seek professional advice and support. But don't give up because the situation is not ideal. There is so much that can still be done, even if your child is picking up the differences between you. Don't lose your focus on what you can achieve and put into practice.

Special Time for Older Children

Children of all ages can benefit from getting your undivided attention during Special Time, even though the term 'Special Time' may sound childish for older kids (seven and over). The key ingredients of Special Time are:

- making time daily to do an activity together – without distraction
- genuinely exploring your child's views and interests
- demonstrating your attention by listening and giving feedback
- avoiding attempts to teach, lecture or reprimand and be the boss
- having fun together.

The process may actually be easier with an older child, whose interests will be more developed than a toddler's. So try applying the Special Time principles to structured activities like those below. Some will take place away from home, which will probably involve some planning.

- swimming
- horse riding
- walks

- movies
- snooker

- fishing
- bike rides
- football (watching a match he is playing in, taking him to matches, joining in)
- shopping till you drop
- computer games

Schoolwork

You could even include schoolwork in Special Time, as long as you don't fall into the seductive trap of trying to correct, improve, criticise, etc. Remember, Special Time is conflict-free time. Only work with those aspects of schoolwork that your child actually likes.

- Find ten minutes daily to check out what your child has been taught today. Talk over what he may have found of interest. Find out if there is anything you can do to stimulate that interest or help him with. It pays to be upbeat and positive about what he is learning. Give him a chance to show how much he knows before you step in with your ideas.

- Go out of your way to praise improvements in your child's work. Go through his exercise books and find something to single out for praise. Notice when handwriting is neater. Pick up when marks are higher. Find things to praise in his work that the teacher may have missed. Remember, the older the child the more important it becomes to be as specific as possible in your praise.

- Don't take 'nothing' for an answer. Be more persistent than usual in finding out what is happening at school. 'C'mon, you must remember something – what's the most interesting thing you can remember from today?' Go carefully, though. Probe with warmth and humour. Show you're not going to be fobbed off quickly and you're genuinely interested, but that you won't leap to criticise him.

Friends

This is another key area for older children because they are still learning about making, keeping and losing friends. They won't have sorted it all out yet, so there is plenty of scope for sensitive and genuine interest. But be careful you respect your child's privacy.

- Get into the habit of remembering the details about his friends. Surprise your child by checking out how things are going with David or Victoria. Listen without jumping in with advice, unless asked.

- Whether you like it or not, accept that older children don't want you around! This need to be separate has to be respected. But in my experience, if you are willing to let your child guide you on how much he wants to tell you about his problems with friends or worries about not having any, then the safer he will feel about opening up to you.

Mealtimes

As children get older they like to please themselves more as far as mealtimes are concerned. You may or may not be flexible on this question. But mealtimes are an important meeting point and there are real benefits in insisting that the whole family gets together around the meal table at least once a week.

TIPS FOR SUCCESS

- Get some positive feedback. Try asking everyone around the table to say a few words about one positive thing that happened for them that day or week.

- Keep in touch. Check out some issue or incident that you were told or heard about before, and ask, 'What's happening now...?'

- Do a bit of planning. Make sure that you can rely on the other adults and siblings to be upbeat and positive at family mealtimes. Don't expose yourselves to lots of divisions and grumbles when the aim is to unite everyone.

Remember in general:

- ADD kids love activities with plenty of stimulation and action.

- Never show them up in front of their mates. Be prepared to make yourself scarce if this is on the cards.

- Expect your efforts to be rejected fairly often. Don't give up. Adolescents can be up and down in their moods. How they feel about you and the world in general can change rapidly.

- You need to persist to get your 'I *am* interested' message across. Older children scrutinise more closely whether you mean what you say. If you give up too quickly they may assume your interest wasn't genuine.

Frequently asked questions

Q: '*My son acts really stupid at times when we're out, taking risks and so on. How should I handle this if it is meant to be a fun, "boss-free" time together?*'

A: This is bound to happen on occasions. So you need to be clear about the minimum expectations you have on behaviour. If you have major worries about what might go wrong and spoil the time together, talk them over before you leave home. While you're out, try to ignore as much of his risk-taking as you feel comfortable with. But if things get out of hand, then the show is over and it's back home.

Q: '*Trying to get our child to participate in special activities with either my husband or me causes flare-ups and rows as a family – is there any point in pushing it?*'

A: No. If your attempts are dividing the family instead of bringing you together, pause for thought. Reflect on how long it has been this way. Decide if you have a serious problem in the quality of your relationship with your child. If so, it might be wise to seek advice from someone outside the family. Talking to a professional such as a child psychologist or family therapist about these issues might bring a new perspective.

FINAL TIP FOR SUCCESS

- As old as he or she may be, your child is never so mature or so autonomous that you have lost the opportunity to have Special Time together. Be a nuisance if necessary, but make that time together happen. Make it positive and fun – and praise, praise and praise again.

Support Groups

UK

ADD Information Services

A charitable body that has links with over 150 support groups in the UK. A full list is available on request. The service offers advice to parents, young people and professionals. It also organises and coordinates seminars and conferences for parent support groups and professional organisations. Every autumn the service holds an international conference for parents and professionals, which is a good forum for finding out what the latest thinking is on ADD.

If you want a book on ADD and cannot find it locally, ADD Information Services has a wide stock of both books and videos, available by mail order. A large SAE gets you details and information.

Mrs Andrea Bilbow
PO Box 340
Edgware
Middlesex HA8 9HL
Tel: 020 8905 2013 Fax: 020 8386 6466
E-mail: iss@compuserve.com

The ADHD Family Support Group

Another source of information and advice aimed at the parents of ADHD and ADD children as well as professionals. Mails a regular newsletter to members. For details, send a large SAE to:

Mrs Gill Mead
1A The High Street
Dilton Marsh
Wiltshire BA13 4DL
Tel: 01373 826045

ADHD North West

If you are living in the North West this is the organisation that can put you in touch with local 'contact parents' and support groups. Contact details:

> Mrs Barbara Worral
> Tel: 01524 822887
> E-mail: worral@addnorthwest.u-net.com

Contact a Family

A charitable organisation that puts parents of children with ADD and ADHD in touch with each other. The service also advises on other organisations that can help.

> 170 Tottenham Court Road
> London W1P 0HA
> Tel: 020 8383 3555

Child Line

Free 24-hour help line for children

> Freephone 0800 1111

Relate

> Herbert Gray College
> Little Church Street
> Rugby
> CV21 3AP
> Tel: 01788 573241
>
> Website: *www.relate.org.uk*

Eire

HADD (Hyperactivity Attention Deficit Disorder)

> Stephanie Mahoney, Dublin
> Tel: 00 353 1 288 9766
> Maeve Daly, Dublin
> Tel: 00 353 1 822 2059.

Australia

ADDISS (ADD Information and Support Services)

> PO Box 1661
> Milton, Queensland 4064
> Tel: 00 61 7 3368 3977

Learning Disabilities Coalition Group

Sydney, New South Wales
Tel: 00 61 2 9542 3390

United States

CHADD (Children and Adults with Attention Deficit Disorder)

National Headquarters
Suite 308
499 NW 70th Avenue
Plantation, FL 33317
Tel: 00 1 305 487 3700

LDA (Learning Disabilities Association)

4156 Library Road
Pittsburgh, PA 15234
Tel: 00 1 412 341 1515

Suggested Reading and Websites

Attention Deficit Disorder and Attention Deficit Hyperactivity Disorder

Consult these books to learn more about the condition, how it is diagnosed and what might be the causes.

Barkley, R.A. (1990) *Attention Deficit Hyperactivity Disorder*. London: Guilford Press.
Russell Barkley is a world-renowned researcher and writer on ADD, and this book has everything you could possibly want of an academic book on the condition.

Barkley, R.A. (1998) 'Attention Deficit Hyperactivity Disorder.' *Scientific American*, September, 44–49.
This gives more information about how the brain is affected in ADD. It is available on the Internet at *www.sciam.com/1998/0998issue/0998barkley.htm*

Green, C. (1995) *Understanding Attention Deficit Disorder*. London: Vermilion.
A good general guide to identifying and understanding ADD. Written by an Australian paediatrician.

Munden, A. and Arcelus, J. (1999) *The ADHD Handbook*. London: Jessica Kingsley Publishers.
Another well-written general guide to ADD, bang up-to-date. Not as parent-friendly as Green's book. Written by two child psychiatrists based in Birmingham, England.

Managing behaviour problems

Gerber, S.W., Gerber, M.D. and Spitzman, R.F. (1990) *Helping the ADD/Hyperactive Child*. New York: Villard Books.
Written by a husband and wife team, this book has lots of tips and ideas about handling and managing ADD. It is clearly written, quite broad in its scope and sympathetic to parents and ADD children alike.

Phelan, T. (1995) *1–2–3 Magic*. Glen Ellyn, ILL: Child Management Inc.
Parents with ADD children recommend this book highly for its handling of defiance. The 'magic' is basically Time Out in a new guise. This is an easy-to-follow

Getting motivated

Robbins, A. (1986) *Unlimited Power.* New York: Simon & Schuster.
Anthony Robbins is the guru of self-motivation. This book is all about creating change in your life. If you like his style, then there are few writers (or speakers) in the same league as Robbins. He is particularly effective on tape – look out for the taped versions of his books, particularly *Unlimited Power.*

Robbins, A. (1986) *Unlimited Power.* New York: Sound Ideas, Simon & Schuster.

Robbins, A. (1991) *Awaken the Giant Within.* New York: Sound Ideas, Simon & Schuster.

Communication skills and family life

Bailey, A. (1997) *TalkWorks.* British Telecom plc. Available via Freephone 0800 800 808.
An easy-to-read little book about communication skills. Published by BT as part of an initiative to promote better communication.

Skynner, R. and Cleese, J. (1983) *Families and How to Survive Them.* London: Methuen.
A definite 'must read' on understanding family relationships.

Smith, M.J. (1975) *When I Say No, I Feel Guilty.* New York: Bantam Books.
The popular classic on being assertive in your communication.

School

Describing the needs of your ADD child to the school can be an uphill struggle. It is a good idea to prepare yourself with some ideas and information that you can tactfully share with teaching staff or suggest they read.

Attwood, T. (1997) *ADD: Practical Activities in School.* Oxford: Winslow Press.
Written by a teacher, this book is about the needs of ADD children in the classroom and about strategies to help.

Cooper, P. and Ideus, K. (1996) *Attention Deficit/Hyperactivity Disorder, A Practical Guide for Teachers.* London: David Fulton Publishers.
This book, written for teachers, provides practical advice on managing the effects of ADD in the classroom.

Books for ADD children

This looks like a growing market. My advice is to check out before buying – you know best what kind of books appeal to your kids. If in doubt, order through your local library. Many titles come from the States. Here are a few that have proved popular with children I have worked with:

Books for ADD children

This looks like a growing market. My advice is to check out before buying – you know best what kind of books appeal to your kids. If in doubt, order through your local library. Many titles come from the States. Here are a few that have proved popular with children I have worked with:

Gordon, M. (1993) *I Would If I Could.* New York: GSI Publications.

Moser, A. (1994) *Don't Rant and Rave or Wednesday.* Missouri: Landmark Editions Inc.

Quinn, P. and Stern, J. (1991) *Putting on the Brakes: A Young People's Guide to Understanding ADHD.* Washington, DC: A Magination Press.

For adults with ADD

Ramundo, P. and Kelly, K. (1996) *You Mean I'm Not Lazy, Stupid or Crazy? A Self-help Book for Adults with Attention Deficit Disorder.* New York: Scribeness.
Highly recommended, this book written by ADD adults for ADD adults aims to provide practical guidance and support.

Wender, P. (1995) *Attention Deficit Hyperactivity Disorder in Adults.* Oxford: Oxford University Press.
A popular guide for adults with ADD.

ADD on the Internet

Internet websites change all the time. A poor site today can be a great site in two weeks' time. New sites are constantly appearing, and addresses are subject to change. There is no real substitute for doing your own search, but here is my pick of ADD-related sites which is accurate at the time of going to press.

www.ADDapt.co.uk

This is the site for this book. Here you will ind a regularly updated resource on ADD including:

- links to other ADD-related sites
- details of support organisations
- background information on ADD
- extra tips for success and enhancements of ADDapt which emerge from the feedback I get from readers, from my own practice and from other developments in the field
- accounts from parents of their experiences with their ADD children.

www.bbc.co.uk/education/health/chs/hyperact.shtml

The BBC's excellent summary of what ADD is together with some useful UK links.

www.adders.org/infor.htm

A well organised, user friendly and informative site with one or two laughs – all too rare in the ADD world. See for instance 'Things My ADD Child has Taught Me'.

www.chadd.org/

The site of the US-based 'Children and Adults with Attention Deficit/Hyperactivity Disorder' – user-friendly and informative.

ww.add.org/

The site of the US-based National Attention Deficit Disorder Association – very comprehensive.

http://add.tqn.com/health/add/msubuk.htm

About.com's list of UK-based ADD sites.

www.simsue.force9.co.uk/index.htm

The site of ADDrift – a UK-based support group for parents and people with ADD.

Subject Index

accept that ADD has changed the lives of you and your child 34
ADD (Attention Deficit Disorder)
  Alternative Parenting Techniques *see* ADDapt
  books on 161
    for adults with ADD 162
    for children 162–3
  children: can't do? won't do? 144
  differences in symptoms 12–13
  drug debate 23–4
  and hyperactivity 11
  = inattention + impulsiveness 10–11
  on the Internet 163–4
  and medication 21–4
  parents: can't do? won't do? 144
  what you need to know 13–15
ADDapt (ADD Alternative Parenting Techniques) 17–20
  and being in command and under control 146
  and developing new skills 146
  four Golden Rules 27, 28
  four principles 25
  and getting closer to your child 145
  how does it work? 25–6
  as long-term 145
  and medication 21, 22, 24
  motivators 45–9
  and the problem of change 33–4
  programme
    step 1 keeping on task 45–9
    step 2 who's the boss? (taking control) 51–63
    step 3 Home Points System (HPS): Part 1 65–73
    step 4 praise 75–81
    step 5 tackling attention-seeking 83–92
    step 6 secret of commands 93–101
    step 7 task wars 103–9
    step 8 mastering things-to-do 111–17
    step 9 Home Points System (HPS): Part 2 119–25
    step 10 Time Out for difficult behaviours Part 1 127–34
    step 11 Time Out for difficult behaviours Part 2 135–41
    step 12 putting it all together 143–8
  what does it do? 25–8
  what it expects from you 27–8
  why it will work for you 18–19
ADD Information Services 157

ADHD (Attention Hyperactivity Deficit Disorder) 11
ADHD Family Support Group 157
ADHD North West 158
adults with ADD, books for 162
alternative parenting techniques *see* ADDapt
attention-seeking, tackling 83–92, 103
  CLOSE down 89
  extra things to do 92
  frequently asked questions 91
    how do I keep ignoring a determined child? 91
    how do I know if communication is improving? 91
  and negative-attention trap 84
  pitfalls and new approaches 90
  tips for success 88, 92
  what to ignore and what *not* to ignore 86–8
ADDISS (ADD Information and Support Services, Australia) 158
attention skills *see* positive-attention skills
awash with praise exercise 78

backsliding, beware of 38
bad behaviour, no rewards for 85
behaviour modification therapy 147
blame, you are not to 30–2

boost your motivation
    system 46–8
boss, becoming the (taking
    control) 51–63
bribes and rewards 109
building-the-positives
    exercise 49

CHADD (Children and
    Adults with Attention
    Deficit Disorder, US)
    159
Chair (in Time Out) 129,
    131, 132–3, 136–8,
    139
change
  and the basics that you
    need to have in place
    right now 34–5
  being prepared to (Golden
    Rule No. 2) 33–6
  decisions exercise on 36
  expecting resistance from
    ADD children to 35
  problem of, and ADDapt
    33–4
Child Line 158
CLOSE down 89, 136
  1. Cut off conversation 89
  2. Look away 89
  3. Offer no reaction 89
  4. Switch off smiles 89
  5. End when you're ready
    89
closer to your child, getting
    145
command, being in 146
commands
  to avoid 95–8
    'flooded' 96
    'let's' and 'we'll' 97
    question 97
    vague 96
  clarify the message 93–5

delivering effective
    93–101, 103
  during Special Time,
    cutting out 58
  frequently asked questions
    99–101
    isn't this dominating
    and bossy? 99
    my child gets upset with
    the 'new' me 99
    what about negotiation
    and listening to
    children? 100
  pitfalls and new
    approaches 98
  tips for success 97, 99,
    101
  three key guidelines to
    issuing 95
communication skills and
    family life, books on
    162
consistency and ADDapt 27
  with each other 42
  as Golden Rule No. 4
    41–2
  in how you apply ADDapt
    42
  in what you say and do
    41–2
Contact a Family 158
control
  establishing 51–4, 146
  issue of 52–4
  regaining 137
  and Special Time for
    young children 54–6
consulting and telling 114
conversation, cut off (in
    CLOSE down sequence)
    89
criticism, hidden cost of 76

cut off conversation (in
    CLOSE down sequence)
    89

decisions exercise on
    change 36
demotivators 46
  potential 47
developing new skills 146
Dexadrine 21
difficult behaviours, list
    130–1
disciplining, be prepared to
    give up your old ways of
    35
discuss things-to-do
    schedule with your child
    114
Dominic (aged 7) and
    Martine (his mother)
    105–6, 113–14, 115

encouragement and
    ADDapt 25
end when you're ready (in
    CLOSE down sequence)
    89
exercises
  awash-with-praise 78
  building the positives 49
  decisions 36
  motivators 48
  positive-attention skills 63
  resolutions 39
  spotting-success 77
expert help 147
explanation and ADDapt
    25
extra credit 68
eye contact, no 136

failing and succeeding with
    things-to-do 104

false beliefs about ADD
29–30

final draft of things-to-do
schedule 114–15

'flooded' commands, avoid
96

fresh start, making 107

friends 154

Golden Rules of ADDapt
No. 1 ' Don't beat
yourself up!' 29–32
No. 2 'Be prepared to
change' 33–6
No. 3 'Stick with it and be
patient' 37–9
No. 4 'Be consistent' 41

Grant family 22
Harry (aged 6) 9–10, 12
Helen (Harry's mother) 9,
11, 22

guilt and ADDapt 29–30
how to stop feeling guilty
32

HADD (Dublin) 158

Home Points System (HPS)
65–73, 75, 103, 116,
119–25
Part 1 65–73
frequently asked
questions 72
is my child too young
to understand am
HPS? 72
should I include my
other children in
the HPS? 72
what if my child
hoards points? 72
will it work? 72
how does it work? 65–6
key actions 66–70
setting up the HPS 66

tips for success 68–9,
71–2
with younger children
72–3
Part 2 119–25
FAQ: do I use the same
ideas with a younger
child? 125
'less-of' behaviours
119–20
targeting 'less-offs'
120–4
key actions 120–4
tips for success 122,
124–5
how to use this book 20

hyperactivity 11

ignoring attention-seeking
86–8, 91, 103

immediate praise 80

impulsiveness 11, 12

inattention 11, 12

inconsistency and ADDapt
41–2

Internet, ADD-related sites
on 164

interrupting behaviour
patterns that lead to
rows 107

Jamie (aged 7) 9, 10, 11,
12, 136–8
Delia and Rick (Jamie's
parents) 136–8

Julie see under Molly

key actions
'less-ofs' 120–4
1. list 'less-ofs' 120
2. make the 'less-ofs'
chart 121–2
3. put it all together
122–4

'more-ofs' 66–70
1. list 'more-ofs' 66–9
2. list the rewards
69–70

things-to-do 112–16
1 list things-to-do 112
2 pick an easy one 113
3 draw up the schedule
113–14
4 discuss it with your
schedule 114
5 make a final draft
114–15
6 target the rest of
things-to-do 115–16

Time Out 130–1, 133–4
1. read the Time Out
recipe 130
2. list difficult
behaviours 130–1
3. read Step 11 133–4

LDA (Learning Disabilities
Association, US) 159

Learning Disabilities
Coalition Group
(Sydney) 158

'less-of' behaviours
119–20, 121
key actions 120–4
targeting 120–4

'let's' and 'we'll' phrases,
avoid 97

letting the child take the
lead 61

listening and negotiation
100

list things-to-do 112

look away (in CLOSE down
sequence) 89

managing behaviour
problems, books on
161

mealtimes 155
medication and ADD 21–4
  and ADDapt 21, 22, 24
  debate on 23–4
  how ADD has affected
    your child 22
  limitations 21–2
  what medication can do
    21, 24
  what medication can't do
    24
mixed messages, clarifying
  93–5
Molly (aged 5) 9, 10, 11,
  12
  and Julie (Molly's mother)
    52–3, 56
'more-of' behaviours 66,
  67
motivation, books on 162
motivators 45–9, 107, 108
  boost your motivation
    system 46–8
  exercise 48
  potential 46

nagging 105
naughty behaviour and
  Special Time 59–60
negative-attention trap 84
negotiation and listening
  100

offer no reaction (in
  CLOSE down
  sequence) 89
older children, Special Time
  for 153–6
overheard praise 79

parenting techniques,
  alternative 17–20
parents
  avoiding blame 30–2

can't do? won't do? 144
Golden Rules for see
  Golden Rules of
  ADDapt
how to stop feeling guilty
  32
partnership, working in
  149–50
  frequently asked questions
    150–1
  what if both of us feel
    defeated at the same
    time? 150–1
  what if my partner
    won't support me in
    ADDapt? 151
patience and ADDapt 27
  as Golden Rule No. 3
    (sticking with it) 37–9
  persistence 37–9
  resolutions exercise 39
pitfalls and new approaches,
  in tackling
  attention-seeking 90
play, and Special Time
  54–6
plea commands, avoid 98
positive-attention skills 56
  check your (exercise) 63
  develop, during Special
    Time 57
positives, building the
  (exercise) 49
praise and ADDapt 26,
  75–81, 103, 108
  awash with praise exercise
    78
  and building self-esteem
    78–9
  facts about 75–6
  frequently asked questions
    80
  I'm doing all the giving
    80

praise him for what he
    isn't doing? 80
  what about the other
    kids? 80
  and hidden cost of
    criticism 76
  immediate 80
  overheard 79
  and rewarding good
    behaviour 77
  spotting-success exercise
    77
  tips for success 79–80, 81
  as valuable to your child
    76–7
problem things-to-do 112
putting it all together
  143–8

question commands, avoid
  97
questions
  reducing during Special
    Time 57
  swapping for statements
    58

reaction, offer no (in
  CLOSE down
  sequence) 89
resistance from ADD
  children to change,
  expecting 35
resolutions exercise 39
rewards
  and ADDapt 25, 26, 69
  and bribes 109
  for good behaviour 77,
    85, 91
  no rewards for bad
    behaviour 85, 91
  and HPS 124
Ritalin 13, 21, 22, 52

rows, avoiding the road to
107–8

safety, ensuring
  as guide to when to
    ignore bad behaviour
    86–8
schedule of things-to-do
  113–14
school and ADD, books on
  162
schoolwork 153
self-esteem
  building 78–9
  and nagging 105–6
  and things-to-do 104
Simon (aged 10) 9, 10, 11
skills, developing new 146
smacking, how to avoid
  141
Special Time for young
  children 54–6, 75, 103
  develop positive-attention
    skills during 57–8
  frequently asked questions
    59–62
  how can I find the time
    59
  how long does it take?
    59
  and letting the child
    take the lead 61
  and naughty behaviour
    59, 62
  should I push him into
    it? 62
  what if he doesn't want
    to do anything with
    me? 61
  what if I miss a practice?
    59
  when should we have it?
    61
  how it works 55

setting up 55–6
Special Time for older
  children 153–6
  frequently asked questions
    155–6
  how do I handle my
    child acting stupid
    during fun,
    'boss-free' time?
    155–6
  trying to get our child
    to participate in
    special activities
    causes
family rows 156
  and friends 154
  and mealtimes 155
  and schoolwork 153–4
  tips for success 154, 155,
    156
spontaneity 116
strategy, decide on your
  127–8
succeeding and failing with
  things-to-do 104
success 148
success-spotting exercise 77
suggested reading 161–4
support groups 147–8,
  157–9
switch off smiles (in CLOSE
  down sequence) 89

tantrums 83, 85, 106
  and nagging, vicious circle
    of 106
targeting things-to-do
  111–12, 115–16
task peace 107
task wars 103–9
  frequently asked questions
    109
  give point to ensure
    positive start? 109

isn't that bribery? 109
  and making a fresh start
    107
  and the problem with
    'things-to-do' 103–4
  and task peace 107
  tips for success 109
  vicious circle of tantrums
    and nagging 106
  why are things-to-do hard
    for children? 104–6
telling and consulting 114
'things-to-do' 103–4,
  111–17
  failing and succeeding
    with 104
  frequently asked questions
    116–17
  doesn't this approach
    take the spontaneity
    out of life? 116
  how cool should I be?
  how do I explain this to
    my child? 116
  will my child follow the
    schedule? 116
  mastering 111–17
  key actions 112–16
  problem 112
  targeting 111–12
Time Out for difficult
  behaviours 127–34
  frequently asked questions
    138–40
  can I use Time Out for
    not doing
    something? 139
  how do I cope with
    problems in the
    supermarket etc.?
    139
  how do we manage to
    stick at Time Out?
    140

how do we use Time
      Out in public?138
if Time Out upsets my
      child, patch it up
      afterwards? 140
is Time Out really
      appropriate for older
      children? 140
Part 1 127–34
   decide on your strategy
      127–8
   how the technique
      works 131–3
   key actions 130–1,
      133–4
   Time Out approach
      128–31
   Time Out Chair 129,
      131, 132–3
   Time Out recipe 129
   tip for success 133
Part 2 135–41
   how to avoid smacking
      141
   tips for success 141
treats, no 136
trigger, nagging as a 105

vague commands, avoid 96
vicious circle of tantrums
      and nagging 106

work together 34

Author Index

Angelou, M. 143
Attwood, T. 162

Bailey, A. 162
Barkley, R.A. 161
Buckingham, S. 163

Carnegie, D. 81
Cooper, P. and Ideus, K.
    162

Gerber, S.W., Gerber, M.D.
    and Spitzman, R.F. 161
Gordon, M. 163
Green, C. 161

Moser, A. 163
Munden, A. and Arcelus, J.
    161

Phelan, T. 161

Quinn P. and Stern, J. 163

Ramundo, P. and Kelly, K.
    163

Robbins, A. 162

Skynner, R. ad Cleese, J.
    162
Smith, M.J. 162

Wender, P. 163

Lightning Source UK Ltd.
Milton Keynes UK
18 September 2009

143883UK00001B/21/P